MW00769786

LITTLE PILLOWS

and

MORNING BELLS

LITTLE PILLOWS
or
Good-Night Thoughts for the Little Ones

FRANCES RIDLEY HAVERGAL

SOLID GROUND CHRISTIAN BOOKS
BIRMINGHAM, ALABAMA

Solid Ground Christian Books
2090 Columbiana Rd, Suite 2000
Birmingham, AL 35216
205-443-0311
sgcb@charter.net
http://solid-ground-books.com

LITTLE PILLOWS:
Good-Night Thoughts for the Little Ones

taken from 1883 edition by E.P. Dutton, NY

and

MORNING BELLS:
Waking Thoughts for the Little Ones

taken from 1880 edition by Anson Randolph, NY

by Frances Ridley Havergal (1836-1879)

Solid Ground Classic Reprints

ISBN: 1-932474-25-0

Manufactured in the United States of America

CONTENTS.

HOW "LITTLE PILLOWS" CAME TO BE WRITTEN.

A LITTLE GIRL was away from home on a week's visit. We will suppose her name was Ethel. The first night, when she was tucked up in bed, and just ready for a good-night kiss, I said, "Now, shall I give you a little pillow?"

Ethel lifted her head to see what was under it, and said, "I have got one, Auntie!"

"It was another sort of pillow that I meant to give you; I wonder if you will like it?"

So then Ethel saw it was not a question of feathers and pillow-case; still she did not understand, and so she laughed and said, "Do tell me at once, Auntie, what you mean; don't keep me waiting to guess!"

Then I told her that, just as we wanted a nice soft pillow to lay our heads down upon at night, our hearts wanted a pillow too, something to rest upon, some true, sweet word that we might go to sleep upon happily and peacefully. And that it was a good plan always to take a little text for our pillow every night. So she had one that night, and the next night.

The third night I was prevented from coming up till long after Ethel ought to have been asleep. But there were the bright eyes peeping out robin-red-breast fashion, and a reproachful little voice said, "Auntie, you have not given me any little pillow to-night!"

"Then, do you really care about having the little pillows given you, Ethel?"

"Oh, *of course* I do!" was the answer. She did not seem to think there could possibly be any doubt about it. Certainly the way in which she said that "*of course!*" showed that *she* had no doubt about it!

So it seemed that perhaps other little ones would like to have "little pillows" put ready for every night. For even little hearts are sometimes very weary, and want something to rest upon; and a happy little heart, happy in the love of Jesus, will always be glad to have one of His own sweet words to go to sleep upon.

So here are thirty-one "little pillows," not to be used all at once, nor even two at a time, but one for every night in the month. The little texts are so short, that they will need no learning; but when you have read the explanation, you will be able to keep the text quite safely and quite easily in your mind.

Read the little book before you kneel down to say your evening prayers, because I hope what you read will always remind you of something to pray about. And then, when you lie down and shut your eyes, let your heart rest on the "little pillow" till "He giveth His beloved sleep."

When you have read this little book, another will be ready for you, *Morning Bells*,—little chimes of Bible music to wake you up! Some of them will, I hope, ring in your ears all the day, and help you to go happily and brightly through it, following Jesus at every step.

1.

THE INVITATION.

"Come unto Me."—MATT. xi. 28.

WHAT kind, sweet words for your pillow to-night! Jesus says them to you.

"How am I to know?" Well, they are for every one that is weary and heavy laden. Do not you know what it is to be weary and tired sometimes? Perhaps you know what it is to feel almost tired of trying to be good—weary with wishing you could be better. So, you see, it is to *you* that He says "Come!"

And if you have not yet come, you are heavy laden too, even if you do not feel it; because the burden of sin is heavy enough to sink you down into hell, unless Jesus takes it from you. So it is to *you* that He says "Come!"

And lest you should think He says it to grown-up people only, He said, "Suffer the little children to come unto me." Are you a little child? Then it is to you that He says "Come!"

"If He were here, and if I could see Him, I should like to come." He *is* here, as really and truly as you are. Suppose your mother and you were in a dark room together, and she said, "Come to me!" you would not stop to say, "I would come if I could see you." You would say, "I am coming, mother!" and you would soon feel your way across the room, and be safe by her side. Not seeing her would not make any difference.

Jesus calls you now, this very night. He is here, in this very room. Now, will you not say, "I am coming, Lord Jesus!" and ask Him to stretch out

His hand and help you to come, and draw you quite close to Himself?

Yes, to *Himself*, the blessed, beloved Lord Jesus, who loved you and gave Himself for you, who has waited so patiently for you, who calls you because He wants you to come and be His own little lamb, and be taken up in His arms and blessed. Will you keep Him waiting any longer? Will you not "Come"?

"Will you not come to Him for life?
Why will ye die, oh why?
He gave His life for you, for you!
The gift is free, the word is true!
Will ye not come? Oh why will ye die?"

2.

ACCEPTED.

"Accepted in the Beloved."—EPH. i. 6.

WHO is "accepted in the Beloved"? *You*, if you have come to your heavenly Father, asking him to receive you for Jesus Christ's sake. Dear little one, wanting to know that you are saved and forgiven, take all the beautiful comfort and joy of these words! They are for you just as much as for any grown-up person.

Ask Him *now* to give you faith to believe them for yourself, while you try to understand what they really mean for you.

Suppose a king came and proclaimed among a number of poor children that he would take *any* one to stay with him in his beautiful palace, who really wished to go and asked him to take them. Suppose you heard this, and wished the king would take you. Then the king beckons you, and you venture near; and then the prince royal himself comes and leads you up to his father, and tells you to say what you want, and you say, "I do want to go, please take me!" Will the king break his word and *not* take you? Why, in the first place, he *never* breaks his promise. And then he beckoned you himself, and that was what made you go. And then the prince, who is his beloved son, took your hand and brought you; and would the king send the little one away whom he brought? There can be no mistake about it; he can not have rejected you, and said he will *not* have you, so you *must* be "accepted."

So every one who has come to Jesus, even if only a little girl or boy, is "accepted in the Beloved." Accepted, because God has said, "I will receive you." Accepted, because He Himself has called and drawn you, or you never would have wanted to come. Accepted, because the Beloved One has made the way open for you to come by His own blood, and saves *all* that come unto God by Him. Accepted, not because you were worth God's accepting, but "accepted in the Beloved."

"Safe in the arms of Jesus,
Safe on His gentle breast,
There, by His love o'ershadowed,
Sweetly my soul shall rest.
Hark! 'tis the voice of angels,
Borne in a song to me,
Over the fields of glory,
Over the jasper sea."

3.

THE RED HAND.

"I, even I, am He that blotteth out thy transgressions."—ISA. xliii. 25.

THERE was once a deaf mute, named John. Though he never heard any other voice, he heard the voice of Jesus, knew it, loved it, and followed it.

One day he told the lady who had taught him, partly on his fingers and partly by signs, that he had had a wonderful dream. God had shown him a great black book; and all John's sins were written in it, so many, so black! And God had shown him hell, all open and fiery, waiting for him, because of all these sins. But Jesus Christ had come and put His *red hand*, red with the blood of His cross, all over the page, and the red hand, the *dear* red hand, had blotted all John's sins out; and when God held up the book to the light, He could not see one left!

Now His sweet word to you to-night is, "I, even I, am He that blotteth out your transgressions." Will you believe it? "Only believe," and "according to your faith it shall be unto you." It is no fancy or mere feeling, but God's truth, that Jesus Christ's blood has been shed,—nothing can alter that; and that His precious blood blotteth out our transgressions; as St. Paul says (Col. ii. 14), "Blotting out the handwriting of ordinances that was against us."

And oh how much there is to blot out!—sins that you have forgotten, and sins that you did not think were sins at all, besides those you know of—to-day, yesterday, all the past days of your little life. And all these written in His book!

Do you want to have them blotted out forever? Do you pray, "Blot out mine iniquities?" do you want to know that they are blotted out! Then take His word about it, and just believe that it is true, and true for you—"I *have* blotted out as a thick cloud thy transgressions, and as a cloud thy sins: return unto me, for I have redeemed thee."

"I am trusting Thee, Lord Jesus,
Trusting only Thee;
Trusting Thee for full salvation,
Great and free.

"I am trusting Thee for cleansing
Through the crimson flood;
Trusting Thee to make me holy
By Thy blood."

4.

GOD'S LOVE.

"I have loved you, saith the Lord."—MAL. i. 2.

IS not this a sweet pillow to rest upon to-night? But a pillow is of no use if you only look at it; that does not rest you. You must lay your head down upon it, and then you rest. So, do not only think, "Yes, that is a very nice text"; but believe it, and lay your heart down restfully upon it; and say, "Yes, He loves me!"

How different these words are from what we should have expected! We should have expected God to say, "I will love you, if you will love me." But no! He says, "I *have* loved you." Yes, He has loved you already, poor little restless heart, that wants to be loved! He loves you now, and will love you always.

But you say, "I wish I knew whether He loves *me!*" Why, He *tells* you so; and what could He say more? There it stands—"I have loved you, saith the Lord." It is TRUE, and you need only believe it, and be glad of it, and tell Him how glad you are that He loves you.

But you say, "Yes, I know He loves good people; but I am so naughty!" Then He has a special word for you: "God commendeth His love toward us, in that, while we were yet sinners, Christ died for us." He says nothing about "good people," but tells you that He loved you so much, while you were naughty, that He has sent the Lord Jesus, His own dear, dear Son, to die for you. Could He do more than that?

He says in the same verse (Mal. i. 2), "*Yet* ye say, Wherein hast thou loved us?" *Wherein? O herein!* not that you loved God, but that He loved you, and sent His Son to suffer instead of you.

When you lie down, think how many

answers you can find to that question, "Wherein hast Thou loved us?" See how many proofs of His love you can count up; and then go to sleep on this soft, safe pillow, "I have loved you, saith the Lord!"

"I am so glad that our Father in heaven
Tells of His love in the book He has given,
Wonderful things in the Bible I see;
This is the dearest, that Jesus loves me.

"Oh, if there's only one song I can sing
When in His beauty I see the great King;
This shall my song in eternity be,
'Oh, what a wonder, that Jesus loves me!'"

5.

GOD'S CARE.

"He that keepeth thee will not slumber."
Ps. cxxi. 3.

SOMETIMES little children wake in the night, and feel lonely, and a little bit afraid. This is not because of the darkness; for if others are with them, talking and moving about, they do not mind it at all. But it is the stillness, the strange silence when every body is fast asleep.

Every body? No! The One who loves you best of all is watching you all the time; the One who careth for you never sleeps—"He that keepeth thee will not slumber." He is there all the time, never leaving you one moment alone, never going away at all. It makes no difference to Him that it is very dark, for "the darkness and the light are both alike to Thee." And all through the dark hours He "keepeth thee"; keeps you from every thing that could hurt or even frighten you, so that you may safely and quietly take the sweet sleep He gives you.

He "keepeth thee"; only think who is your Keeper! the mighty God, who can do every thing, and can see every thing. Why need you ever fear with such a Keeper? It is very nice to know that "He shall give His angels charge over thee to keep thee"; but it is sweeter and grander still to think that God Himself keeps us. As if He wanted us to be very sure of it, and to leave us no excuse for ever being afraid any more, He even says it three times over, "He that keepeth thee will not slumber." "Behold, He that keepeth Israel shall neither slumber nor sleep." "The Lord is thy Keeper." What could He say more?

Now what will you say to Him if you wake in the night and feel lonely in the stillness? Will you not recollect what a pillow He has given you to-night to rest upon, and say to Him, "I will trust, and not be afraid"?

"He will take care of you! All through the night
Jesus, the Shepherd, His little one keeps:
Darkness to Him is the same as the light;
He never slumbers and He never sleeps."

6.

WHAT CHRIST BORE FOR US.

"The Lord hath laid on Him the iniquity of us all."—Isa. liii. 6.

WHERE are your sins? Wherever they are, God's terrible punishment must fall. Even if there were only one sin, and that one hidden away down in your heart, God's wrath must find it out, and punish it. It could not escape.

But you know of many more than one; and God knows of more still. And so the great question for you is, Where are they? If He finds them on you, His wrath must fall on you. But if they are put *somewhere else,* you are safe, for He loves you, and only hates your sins. Where can that wonderful "somewhere else" be? To-night's text tells you that God laid them on Jesus. Why did His terrible wrath fall on His beloved, holy Son? Because He had laid our sins on Jesus, and Jesus took them, and was willing to bear them, so that all the dreadful punishment might fall on Him instead of us. Instead of *you*, dear little one!

When the great drops of blood fell down to the ground from His beloved head in Gethsemane, it was because the Lord had laid on Him *your* iniquity. When He hung by His pierced hands and feet upon the cross, alone in the great darkness of God's wrath, it was because He was bearing *your* punishment, because *your* sins were laid upon Him, so that they might not be found upon you, and punished upon you.

Satan will try to persuade you not to believe that *your* sins were laid upon Him, and will try to keep you always doubting it; but God says they were! Which will you believe?

Again look at the solemn question, "Where are your sins?" and then look at Jesus, suffering and dying for you, and answer boldly, "On Jesus! for 'the Lord hath laid on Him the iniquity of us all.'"

"And so He died! And this is why
He came to be a man and die:
The Bible says He came from heaven,
That we might have our sins forgiven.

"He knew how wicked men had been,
He knew that God must punish sin;
So, out of pity, Jesus said,
He'd bear the punishment instead."

7.

PEACE THROUGH BLOOD.

"Peace through the blood of His cross."
COL. i. 20.

IF you had been disobedient and naughty to your dear mother, you would feel that there was something between you and her, like a little wall built up between you. Even though you knew she loved you and went on doing kind things for you as usual, you would not be happy with her; you would keep away from her, and it would be a sorrowful day both for her and for you. For there would be no sweet, bright *peace* between her and you, and no pleasant and untroubled peace in your own heart.

The Lord Jesus knew that it was just like this with us, that there was something between us and God instead of peace, and this something was sin. And there never could be or can be any peace with God while there is sin, so of course there never could be any real peace in our hearts. We could never take away this wall of sin; on the contrary, left to ourselves, we only keep building it higher and higher by fresh sins every day. And God has said, that "without shedding of blood there is no remission," that is, no forgiveness, no taking away of sins. Now what has Jesus Christ done for us? He has made peace through the blood of His cross. He is the Lamb of God that taketh away the sin of the world; and the sin was what hindered peace.

Look at His precious blood shed to take away your sins! Do you see it, do you believe it? Then there is nothing between you and God, for that bleeding Hand has broken down the wall; the blood has made peace, and you may come to your heavenly Father and receive His loving forgiveness, and know that you have peace with God, through Jesus Christ our Lord.

"Precious blood that hath redeemed us,
All the price is paid!
Perfect pardon now is offered,
Peace is made.

"Precious blood, whose full atonement
Makes us nigh to God!
Precious blood, our song of glory,
Praise and laud!

"Precious, precious blood of Jesus,
Ever flowing free!
Oh believe it, oh receive it,
'Tis for thee!"

8.

"WHITER THAN SNOW."

"Whiter than snow."—Ps. li. 7.

BUT snow is whiter than any thing else! Especially if you saw it glittering in the sunshine on the top of a high mountain, where no dust can ever reach it. Mortal eyes have seen something as white as snow, for the raiment of the angel of the resurrection was "white as snow"; and the shining raiment of the Lord Jesus on the Mount of Transfiguration was "exceeding white as snow." But what can be made "whiter than snow"?

"Wash *me*, and *I* shall be whiter than snow!" What, *me?* my naughty, sinful self? my soul so stained with sin, that I can not make it or keep it clean at all? Yes, "*I* shall be whiter than snow" if God washes me.

But water will not do this, and tears will not do it. Only one thing can do it, but that does it surely and thoroughly. "The blood of Jesus Christ His Son cleanseth us from all sin."

This is "the fountain opened for sin and for uncleanness"; and ever since the precious blood was shed, it has always been open. It is open now, this very evening, ready for you to be washed in it, and made "whiter than snow."

Do not stop short at thinking a little about it, but go to your heavenly Father, and ask Him to wash you in the precious blood of Christ.

Be *willing* to be *really* washed. Do not be like some little children, who do not wish to have a clean white frock put on, because they know they can not go and play in the dirt. Be willing not to go back to the dirt any more.

And then *let* Him wash you; do not just say the words, and get up from your knees, and think no more of it; but put your very heart into His hands, and look at the precious blood of Jesus, and wait and ask Him to show you how really it was shed for you, and how really it cleanses from all sin. And then you will be ready, like the Samaritan, to fall down at Jesu's feet, "giving Him thanks" for having washed even you.

"Precious, precious blood of Jesus,
Let it make thee whole!
Let it flow in mighty cleansing
O'er thy soul.

"Though thy sins are red like crimson,
Deep in scarlet glow,
Jesu's precious blood can make them
White as snow."

9.

ASKING.

'Ask what I shall give thee."—II. CHRON. i. 7.

THERE had been a grand day in Israel. The young King Solomon had spoken to all the people, and to all the great men and captains and governors, and they had followed him to the tabernacle of the Lord, and he had gone up to the brazen altar which Bezaleel had made nearly five hundred years before, and had offered a thousand burnt-offerings. "In that night," when it was all over, and Solomon was quiet and alone, "did God appear unto Solomon, and said unto him, Ask what I shall give thee." And Solomon took God at His word, and asked at once for what he felt he wanted most. And God kept his word, and gave him at once what he asked, and promised him a great deal more besides.

This is the message to you to-night, "Ask what I shall give thee."

Think what you most want, and ask for that, for Jesus Christ's sake. You need not, like Solomon, ask for only one thing; you want many things, and you may ask for them all. And God will give—He always does give to the real askers—more than you ask, more than you ever thought of asking.

Perhaps you say, "I don't know what to ask." Then begin by asking Him to show you by His Holy Spirit what you really want, and to teach you to ask for it.

Then you say, "Will He give me whatever I ask?" Well, if you ask something which is not good for you, He loves you too much to give you that! but He will give you something better. But if you ask for something that He has promised to give, you may be quite certain He will give it you. Remind your heavenly Father of His promises, as Solomon did (ver. 9). And you may ask and expect the answer at once, like Solomon, who said, "*Now*, O Lord God!" and "Give me *now!*"

Then listen to God's message, and now, this very evening, ask Him for some of His promised gifts. And when you lie down, try to think of the different things which He has promised, and which you want, and turn every thought into the prayer, "Give me *now*—for Jesus Christ's sake."

"Thou art coming to a King,
Large petitions with thee bring;
For His grace and power are such,
None can ever ask too much."

10.

GOD'S BENEFITS.

"Forget not all His benefits."—Ps. ciii. 2.

IF some kind friend made you a present of twenty dollars to buy all sorts of things with, would you not feel rather hurt if he thought it necessary to say to you, "Do not forget that I gave you this"? Of course you would not forget, you could not possibly be so ungrateful. But what if, after all, you *had* forgotten, and had all your nice things around you without ever recollecting him, would it not touch your heart if he came again and said very gently, "Do not forget"?

I need not tell you Who and what I mean. You know! Have you been forgetting all His benefits, forgetting to thank Him for them, just as if they had all come of themselves? Oh, ask

Him now to forgive you this sin of forgetfulness, for Jesus Christ's sake! But now that He has reminded you and forgiven you, ask Him for the Holy Spirit to help you to recollect His benefits instead of forgetting them.

"His benefits" means all the good things He has done for you, and all the good things He has given you. Try to count up "His benefits" of this one day; and then think of those of yesterday, and last week, and all the year, and all your life since you were a little baby! You will soon find that there are more than you can count, and you will begin to see how very much you have to thank Him for.

And then recollect His still greater benefits—the great gift of Jesus Christ Himself to be your Saviour and Redeemer, and the great gift of salvation through Him, and all His promises of grace and glory!

David speaks of "the multitude of

His tender mercies," and Isaiah tells of "the multitude of His loving-kindnesses." Are not these true and beautiful words? Will you not turn them into a song of thanksgiving, and say, "Bless the Lord, O my soul, and forget not all his benefits: Who crowneth thee with loving-kindness and tender mercies!"

"Now my evening praise I give;
Thou didst die that I might live;
All my blessings come from Thee,
Oh how good Thou art to me!

"Thou, my best and kindest Friend,
Thou wilt love me to the end;
Let me love Thee more and more,
Always better than before."

11.

WILLING AND DOING.

"It is God which worketh in you, both to will and to do of His good pleasure."—PHIL. ii. 13.

RATHER a hard "pillow" to-night, you think! But it is what will make many hard things quite easy for you.

Have you not found it hard to be good? hard to keep from saying something naughty that you wanted to say? very hard to keep down the angry feeling, even if you did not say the angry word? hard to do a right thing, because you did not at all like doing it, and quite impossible to make yourself wish to do it? You asked God to help you to do it, and He did help you; but did you ever think of asking Him to make you *like* to do it?

Now, this is just what is meant by God's "working in you to *will.*" It means that He can and will undertake the very thing which you can not manage. He can and will "take your will, and work it for you"; making you want to do just what He wants you to do; making you like the very things that He likes, and hate just what He hates.

It is always easy to do what we like doing; so, when we have given up our will to Him, and asked Him to work it for us, it makes every thing easy. For then we shall *want* to "do according to His good pleasure," and we shall be very happy in it; because trying to please Him will not be fighting against our own wills, when God has taken them and is working them for us.

Do you not see what happy days are before you if you will only take God at His word about this? Only try Him, and you will see! Tell Him that you have found you can not manage your will yourself, and that now you will give it up to Him, and trust Him, *from now,* not only to work in you to *do,* but to work in you to *will* also, "according to His good pleasure."

> "Take my will, and make it Thine;
> It shall be no longer mine.
>
> "Take my heart, it is Thine own;
> It shall be Thy royal throne."

12.

"THOU KNOWEST."

"O Lord, Thou knowest."—JER. xv. 15.

THIS little text has been a comfort to many a sorrowful child, as well as to older persons. Things are not always bright with the little ones, and they do not always get as much sympathy as they want, because their troubles are not exactly the same sort as those of grown-up people. Has there been something of this kind to-day, dear little one? Have you felt troubled and downhearted, and you could not explain it to any one, and so no one could comfort you because no one understood? Take this little pillow to rest your tired and troubled little heart upon to-night, "Thou knowest!" Thou, Lord Jesus, kind Shepherd of the weary or wandering little lambs, Thou knowest all about it! Thou hast heard the words that made me feel so sad; Thou hast seen just what happened that troubled me; Thou knowest what I could not explain, "Thou understandest my thought;" Thou hast been looking down into my heart all the time, and there is nothing hid from Thee! Thou knowest *all* the truth about it! and Thou knowest all that I can not put into words at all!

Is it not comfort already, just to know that He knows? And is it not enough that he knows? Why, you know that He can do every thing; so, surely, He can make things come right for you (really right, not perhaps what you fancy would be nicest and most right). And you know that He careth (that is, goes on caring) for you; so, if He knows about your trouble, He cares about it too. And He not only cares, but loves, so that He would not have let this trouble touch His dear child,—when He knew about it all the time,—but that He wanted it to be a little messenger to call you to Him to be comforted, and to show you that He is your best Friend, and to teach you the sweetness of saying, "Thou knowest!"

"Jesus is our Shepherd
Wiping every tear;
Folded in His bosom,
What have we to fear?

"Only let us follow
Whither He doth lead;
To the thirsty desert,
Or the dewy mead."

13.

OUR COMFORTER.

"When the Comforter is come."—JOHN xv. 26.

LITTLE children often want comforting. Something troubles you, and the grown-up people do not know, or do not think it is much to be troubled about, and so nobody comforts you, and you feel very sad. Sometimes they try, and yet it does not seem to comfort you. And sometimes you have even "refused to be comforted."

What a beautiful name this is for the Holy Spirit, "The Comforter!" so gentle, so kind, so loving. When He comes He is true to His name, and brings sweet comfort even for the little troubles of His little ones.

Is He come to you? Your heavenly Father has promised to give the Holy Spirit to them that ask Him. So, if you ask, He is sure to give. Then ask that the Holy Spirit may come into your heart, and dwell there always.

Is He come to you? Are you not quite sure whether He has come yet, or not? The rest of this verse tells you how you may know. Jesus said, "When the Comforter is come, He shall testify of me." That means, He will *tell you about Jesus;* He will put thoughts of Jesus into your mind, and love to Jesus into your heart, and He will make you see and understand more about Jesus than you did before. If you are thinking about Him, and glad to hear about Him, and trying to please Him, I think the Comforter is come, and is beginning to testify of Jesus in you.

Is He come to you? Then you will

never be without a Comforter, whatever troubles come; if they are little vexations or disappointments, He can make you see the bright side, and be patient, and trustful, and happy; if they are great troubles, perhaps illness, or some dear one taken away from you, still He can so comfort you, that you will wonder and find out for the first time what a *very* precious gift He is, and what sweet peace can hush your sorrow "when the Comforter is come."

"Our blest Redeemer, ere He breathed
His tender, last farewell,
A Guide, a Comforter, bequeathed,
With us to dwell.

'And His that gentle voice we hear,
Soft as the breath of even,
That checks each fault, that calms each fear,
And speaks of heaven."

14.

THE BLIND MAN.

"What wilt thou that I shall do unto thee?"
LUKE xviii. 41.

ONLY a blind beggar by the wayside? But Jesus of Nazareth stood still when He cried to Him. He could not grope his way among the crowd, but Jesus commanded him to be brought near to Him. He knew why the poor man had cried out, but He would have him tell it to Himself. So He said, "What wilt thou that I shall do unto thee?" Wonderful question, with a wonderful promise wrapped up in it! For it meant that the mighty Son of God was ready to do whatever this poor blind beggar asked. What did he ask? First, just what he most wanted! Not what he supposed he ought to ask, nor what any one had taught him to ask, nor what other people asked; but simply *what he wanted.* Secondly, he asked straight off for a miracle! He never stayed to question whether it was likely or not, nor how Jesus of Nazareth would do it, nor whether it was too much to ask all at once, nor whether the people would think him too bold. He knew what he wanted, and He believed that Jesus of Nazareth could do it, and so he asked, and that was enough.

"And Jesus said unto him, Receive thy sight: thy faith hath saved thee."

And *that* was enough, his prayer of faith, and Christ's answer of power, for "immediately he received his sight." Was that all? did he go back to beg by the wayside? No; he "followed Him, glorifying God." What a change from the cry of only a few minutes before!

Just one thing more is told us in this

lovely little story, "And all the people, when they saw it, gave praise unto God." See what that first cry of "Have mercy on me," so quickly led to! Who would have expected a few minutes before to have seen him with his eyes open, following Jesus, glorifying God, and causing a whole crowd to give praise to God! I think the Lord Jesus says to you to-night, "What wilt *thou* that I shall do unto thee?" What will you answer Him?

"Pass me not, O tender Saviour!
Let me love and cling to Thee;
I am longing for Thy favor,
When Thou comest, call for me.
Even me."

15.

"THIS SAME JESUS."

"This same Jesus."—Acts i. 11.

"JESUS CHRIST, the same yesterday, and to-day, and forever." Yes, the very same to you to-night that He was to the disciples who stood gazing up into heaven, when, having lifted up His hands and blessed them, He went up to the opening gates of glory.

The very same to you to-night that He was to the little children, when He took them up in His arms and blessed them. Not a bit different! Just as kind, just as loving, just as ready to take you up too, and bless you, and keep you always "safe in the arms of Jesus."

The very same to you to-night that He was when He said so lovingly,

"Come unto Me, all ye that labor and are heavy laden, and I will give you rest." Do you not feel that you would have loved him ever so much if you had heard Him say that, and that you would have gone to Him at once, because He was so good and kind? Well, He is "this same Jesus" now. When you lie down, see how many sweet and gracious words and deeds of His you can recollect, and say to yourself with every one, "He is the same now, and the same for me!"

You are not always the same to Him. When He comes and knocks at the door of your heart, you are sometimes ready to open; and sometimes you give Him a cold, short, careless answer; and sometimes no answer at all. But He is always the same to you; always ready to receive you with tender love and pardon when you come to him.

Perhaps you do not feel so happy now as you did one day when you felt that He was very near and gracious, and full of forgiving love to you? What has changed? Only your feelings, not the Lord Jesus. He is always "this same Jesus"; and you may rest on this to-night, and forever.

> "For this word, O Lord, we bless Thee,
> For our Saviour's changeless name;
> Yesterday, to-day, forever,
> Jesus Christ is still the same."

16.

COME AND SEE!

"Come and see."—John i. 39, 46.

THE Lord Jesus said it first. He said it to the two disciples of John who heard that He was the Lamb of God. They knew very little about Him, but they followed Him. Perhaps they would not even have ventured to speak, but, "Jesus turned, and saw them following," and spoke to them. Then they asked Him where He dwelt, and He said, "Come and see!"

Philip said it next. He had found Christ himself, and at once he told his friend Nathanael about Him, and said, "Come and see!"

Is it not said to you to-night? Oh "Come and see" Jesus! Come and kneel down before Him, and look up into His glorious and loving face, and see what a lovely and precious Saviour He is! Come and see how kind and good He is! Come and see how ready He is to receive you, to take you up in His arms and bless you. Come and see what He has done for you; see how He loved you and gave Himself for you; how He lived, and suffered, and bled, and died for you! Come and see what gifts He has for you, forgiveness and peace, His Spirit and His grace, His joy and His love! Come and see where He dwelleth—see that He is ready to come in and dwell with you, to make your little heart His own dwelling-place. Oh if I could but persuade you to "come and see!" There is no other sight so glorious and beautiful. Will you not come?

When you have come, when you can say like Philip, "We have found Him!" and like St. Paul, "We see Jesus," will you not say to some one else, "Come and see"? You will wish every one else to come to Him, and you have His word to bid you try to bring them: "Let him that heareth say, Come!" Will you not say "Come" to some little friend or brother or sister, or to any one to whom He makes you wish to say it? There is no sweeter invitation for you to give than "Come and see!" the

"Jessie, if you only knew
What He is to me,
Surely you would love Him too,
You would "come and see."

"Come, and you will find it true,
Happy you will be!
Jesus says, and says to you,
'Come! Oh come to me!'"

17.

TELLING JESUS.

"Told Him all things."—Mark vi. 30.

WHEN you have been out for a day, what do you look forward to as you come home in the evening? Why do you run so eagerly into the house, and look so bright? You want to tell "all about it" to some one whom you love,—father, or mother, or brothers and sisters; and you can hardly talk fast enough to pour it all out. You begin at the beginning, and tell every thing (if they will only let you stay up long enough),—the pleasures and the mishaps, what has been done, or what has been said.

When each day is over, and you go up to bed, what do you tell Jesus? Do you tell Him every thing too? Perhaps you do not tell Him any thing at all; or perhaps you only tell Him of something that you have done wrong, and are sorry for; you never thought of such a thing as telling Him *every thing!* Yet He loves you better than the dear ones down-stairs, who listened to all your little stories.

When the apostles had been away, they "gathered themselves together unto Jesus, and told Him all things, both what they had done, and what they had taught." Can you not fancy the gentle, gracious Master listening to every thing so kindly, so patiently, letting them tell Him all their mistakes and all their success, all that had made them glad and all that had made them sorry? And can you not fancy the disciples sitting at His feet, and looking up into His face, and seeing how interested He was in all they had done, and not wishing to keep any thing back from such a dear Master, and finding their own love to Him growing warmer and brighter for this sweet hour of talk with Him! How different if they had just said a few cold words to Him, and never *told* Him any thing! Try this to-night! It will be such a help, such a comfort, and before long you will find it such a joy to tell Jesus every thing!

"Tell Him all the failures,
Tell Him all the sins;
He is kindly listening
Till His child begins.

"Tell Him all the pleasures
Of your merry day,
Tell Him all the treasures
Crowning all your way."

18.

CHRIST'S DEATH FOR US.

"Our Lord Jesus Christ, who died for us."
I THESS. v. 9, 10.

DIED for us? Who else ever did as much for you? who else ever loved you as much? Only think now, what it really means, because it is really true; and surely it is most horribly ungrateful, when one for whom such a great thing has been done does not even think about it.

You would think it hard to be punished for some one else's fault; but this is exactly what your dear Saviour did,—let Himself be punished for your fault instead of you.

Suppose some cruel man were going to cut off your leg, what would you think if your brother came and said, "No; chop mine off instead!" But that would not be dying for you. And "our Lord Jesus Christ *died*" for you.

It was the very most he could do, to show His exceeding great love to you. He was not obliged to go through with it; He might have come down from the cross any moment. The nails could not have kept Him there an instant longer than He chose; His love and pity were the real nails that nailed Him fast to the cross till the very end, till He could say, "It is finished," till He "*died* for us."

It was not only because He loved His Father that He did it, but because He loved us; for the text goes on—"Who died for us, that, whether we wake or sleep, we might live together with Him." So He loved us so much that He wanted us to live together with Him; and as no sin can enter His holy and beautiful home, He knew our sins must be taken away before we could go there. And only blood could take away sin, only death could atone for it; and so He bled, that we might be washed in His most precious blood; He died, "that, whether we wake or sleep, we might live together with Him."

"There is a word I fain would speak,
Jesus died!
O eyes that weep, and hearts that break.
Jesus died!
No music from the quivering string
Could such sweet sounds of rapture bring;
O may I always love to sing,
Jesus died! Jesus died!"

19.

NOTHING, OR EVERY THING?

"Is it nothing to you?"—LAM. i. 12.

THIS was said of a great, great sorrow, which should have touched the heart of every one who passed by and saw it, the terrible troubles that came upon Jerusalem and her children.

But this was also a type of the far more terrible cup of sorrow which the Lord Jesus drank for us, drank it willingly, so that we might drink of the river of His pleasures. Listen! for it is as if He said to you and me, "Is it nothing to you, all ye that pass by? behold and see if there be any sorrow like unto my sorrow!"

"Behold and see" how all His life He was "a Man of sorrows," not having where to lay His head; His own brethren refusing to believe in Him, the wicked Jews hating Him, and over and over again trying to kill Him, and He knowing all the while what awful suffering was before Him.

"Behold and see" Him in the garden of Gethsemane, "being in an agony," and saying, "My soul is exceeding sorrowful, even unto death."

"Behold and see" Him, scourged and spit upon, led as a lamb to the slaughter, and then nailed to the cross;

suffering even unto death, thirsting in the terrible pain, and yet not drinking to still it, and saying in the midst of it all, "My God, my God, why hast Thou forsaken me?" Was ever any sorrow like unto the sorrow that our Lord Jesus Christ went through for love of us? Is it nothing to you? Can you look at it and not care about it? Can you "pass by" and go on just the same as if He had never loved and suffered?

Oh, instead of "nothing," let it be henceforth *every thing* to you! Let it be the reason why you hate sin and why you try to do right; let it be your peace and joy, your strength and your song; let it fill your heart with love and gratitude; let it make you brave and determined to live for Him who suffered and died for you.

"See, oh see, what love the Saviour
Also hath on us bestowed;
How He bled for us and suffered,
How He bare the heavy load.

"On the cross and in the garden
 Oh how sore was His distress!
Is not this a love that passeth
 Aught that tongue can e'er express!"

20.

THE BEAUTY OF THE LORD JESUS.

"Yea, He is altogether lovely."—SONG OF SOL. v. 16.

HE! We do not need to ask "Who?" for these words could only be said of One,—the Beloved One, the Holy One, the Blessed One, the Glorious One! Only of Jesus, *our* Lord Jesus, whom having not seen we love, whom we shall see one day in all His beauty, "when He shall come to be glorified in His saints, and to be admired in all them that believe!" Oh if we could see Him now, as He is at this very moment, sitting at the right hand of the Majesty on high, Himself the very brightness of God's glory, the splendor would be too great, we should fall at His feet as dead, as St. John did, unless He strengthened us to behold His glory. But if He laid His right hand upon us, saying, "Fear not," and we looked again, what should we see? Oh what loveliness! oh what unspeakable beauty! "Fairer than the children of men," and "the chiefest among ten thousand," is our Lord Jesus! And in all the glory He is "this same Jesus"; although His countenance is now as the sun shineth in his strength, there is the gentle smile for His little children, and the tender kindness for the sick ones, and the wonderful, wonderful look of mighty love that would bring the whole world to His feet if they could only see it. And there are scars too, which make His very beauty more beautiful, for they are scars of love. He did not lose the print of the nails when He rose from the grave, and the angels and redeemed ones around Him can see them even now; for even "in the midst of the throne" He is the "Lamb, as it had been slain." So the love has overflowed the glory, and our Lord Jesus is "altogether lovely." *Our* Lord Jesus! Yes, for the Altogether Lovely One has given Himself for us, and given Himself to us; so that even the least of His little ones may look up and say, "This is my Beloved, and this is my Friend!"

"Oh Saviour, precious Saviour,
My heart is at Thy feet;
I bless Thee, and I love Thee,
And Thee I long to meet.

"To see Thee in Thy beauty,
To see Thee face to face,
To see Thee in Thy glory,
And reap Thy smile of grace!"

21.

THE COMING OF THE LORD JESUS.

"Behold, He cometh!"—Rev. i. 7.

DOES this seem a terrible verse? do you wonder why it should be one of the "little pillows," and wish the book had given you a different one to go to sleep upon to-night? Look at it again: "*He* cometh!" Who? Jesus Himself, the "same Jesus" who said, "Come unto Me." You thought it would be so nice to come, if you could only see Him. But you will see Him, for He is coming.

Think of seeing Him come, so beautiful, so glorious, so "altogether lovely"; Him, the very same dear, kind Saviour, who loves the little children, who loves you and has called you! Seeing His very face; the very brow that was crowned with thorns, the very eyes that looked on Peter, the very lips that said such wonderful and gracious things! No longer thinking about Him, and trying to believe on Him, and praying to Him, and wishing for Him, but really seeing Him! Is *this* terrible? Does it not rather seem something to look forward to very much?

Only one thing would make it terrible, and that is, if you will not come to Him now, and will not let Him wash away your sins in His precious blood. Then it would indeed be terrible, for He would never any more say to you "Come!" but only "Depart!"

But you want Him to wash you clean, do you not? and you did try to come to Him? And you believe He means what He says, and really died to save you? Then, oh! shall you not be glad to see Him? What if now the cry were heard, "Jesus is coming!" Your heart would beat quick, but I think it would be with gladness, not with terror. Jesus is coming! Would you not go forth to meet Him? Jesus is coming! Could any thing be happier news? I think we shall not think much about the sound of the trumpet, and the clouds of glory, and all the holy angels that come with Him; we shall "see Jesus," and hear His own voice, and that will fill our eyes and our hearts forever.

"Thou art coming, O my Saviour!
  Thou art coming, O my King!
In Thy beauty all-resplendent,
In Thy glory all-transcendent,
  Well may we rejoice and sing!"

22.

MY KING!

"Now then do it."—II SAM. iii. 18.

DAVID had been anointed king over Israel long before, but the people did not own him while Saul was their king. Then after long wars and troubles Saul was killed. But still it was only Judah who followed David; and for seven years and a half Israel held back. At last Abner said to the elders of Israel, "Ye sought in times past for David to be king over you, *Now then do it!*" And they did it.

Now God has long ago anointed the Lord Jesus to be our King, but is He your own king yet? is He reigning in your heart? Have you ever come to Him and said, "Thou shalt be *my* King, Lord Jesus"?

Perhaps, like the Israelites, you have "sought in times past for Him to be King over you"; you have been wishing He would come and reign, and put down all the wrong tempers and naughty thoughts which master you sometimes like strong rebels. Do you really wish it? Then that wish is like a messenger sent to prepare the way before Him; but wishing is not enough —"Now then *do* it!" Now, this very night, before you go to sleep, tell the dear Saviour, who has been waiting, to come and set up His kingdom of peace and joy in your heart, that He shall be your King *now!* Own Him your King at once; say to Him reverently, and lovingly, and with all your heart, "Jesus, my King!"

Then, when Satan tries to get back to his old throne in your heart, tell him it can not be his ever again, for you have given it up to your King Jesus, and that He is to reign there always now; and that He will not give it up, but will fight for you, and put down all the rebels.

Do not say, "Oh yes, I should like this very much!" and just go to sleep as usual; but "now then *do* it!" and then lie down with the happy thought, "My King!"

"Reign over me, Lord Jesus!
 Oh make my heart Thy throne!
It shall be Thine, dear Saviour,
 It shall be Thine alone.

"Oh come and reign, Lord Jesus;
 Rule over every thing!
And keep me always loyal
 And true to Thee, my King!"

23.

CALLED BY NAME.

"I have called thee by thy name."
ISA. xliii. 1.

LOOK out, if it is a clear night, and see the stars sparkling all over the sky. You can not count them; no one can, because there are more than eyes or telescopes have ever reached. But "He calleth them all by names," knows every one separately. And yet, though He has all those wonderful worlds of light in His hands, and "bringeth out their host by number," He turns to say to each of His poor little weak children on this dark earth, "I have called thee by thy name." He knows your name; you are not merely one of the rest to Him, you are ——— to Him. Take a pencil and write your own name there, it will be perfectly true!

That name was given you in His presence, and by His minister, when you were baptized, in obedience to our Saviour's command; that very name is a token that you are called to be His own child. God knows it, and calls you by it.

But He has done more than this. Why do you care to read this little book every night? why do you care to hear about the things which are "not seen,"—about Jesus, and salvation, and heaven? What is it that seems like a little voice within, persuading you to seek and love Jesus? That is God's own voice in your heart, calling you by name! For you know it is to *you*, because it is only in your own heart; no one else hears it, no one else even knows of it. When He calls thus, listen, and see what else He has to say to you: "Fear not; for I have redeemed thee,

I have called thee by thy name; thou art mine!"

"Jesus is our Shepherd,
For the sheep He bled;
Every lamb is sprinkled
With the blood He shed.

"Then on each He setteth
His own secret sign;
'They that have My Spirit,
These,' saith He, 'are mine.'"

24.

MY JEWELS.

"That day when I make up my jewels."
MAL. iii. 17.

"MY jewels!" God tells us who they are—"Every one that feared the Lord, and that thought upon His name." Then if you fear the Lord, and think upon His name, you are one of His jewels, and all that you are going to read about them is for you, and means *you.*

"My jewels!" They are His "special treasure" (see margin), His very own, dearer than all other treasures to Him. We see how very precious they are to Him by the price He paid for them. For every one of them has been purchased, not with silver and gold (all the silver and gold in the world would not have been enough to purchase one of them), but with the precious blood of Christ. That was the greatest thing God had to give, and He gave it for them.

God has found and chosen His jewels, and He will never lose them. Every one of them is kept safe in the casket of His everlasting love. He does not mean to hide them away, and be ashamed of them; for He says they shall "be a crown of glory in the hand of the Lord, and a royal diadem in the hand of thy God." They are not all the same, jewels are of many different colors and sizes; but the day is coming when He will make them up,—when they will all be gathered together in His treasury, and shine together in His glorious crown, and not one will be forgotten, or overlooked, or lost, for every one is "precious in His sight."

Is it not a grand thing to be one of God's jewels? How very wonderful that He should give such a beautiful name to His poor, sinful, worthless children, and set such shining hopes before them! Ought we not to try to walk worthy of this high and holy calling?

"Sons of Zion, ye are precious
In your heavenly Father's sight;
Ye are His peculiar treasure,
And His jewels of delight.

"Sought and chosen, cleansed and polished,
Purchased with transcendent cost,
Kept in His own royal casket,
Never, never to be lost."

25.

ALWAYS MORE!

"He giveth more grace."—JAS. iv. 6.

YES, always more! And if He has given any at all, it is a certain proof that He will give more; for over and over again the Lord Jesus said, "Whosoever hath, to him shall be given." So, if He has given you a little grace, just enough to wish for more, you shall have more; and then when He has given you more, that will be the very reason why you may expect more still. Is it not nice to be always looking forward to "grace for grace"?

Then, as you grow older, and the little vessel grows larger, He will keep on pouring more grace into it. You will outgrow many things, but you will never outgrow this rich and precious supply.

"He giveth more grace" than we ask. If He had given us only what we asked, we should never have had any at all, for it is His grace that first of all makes us wish, and teaches us to ask for it. And He says, "Open thy mouth wide, and I will fill it." Then open it wide! ask Him to fill you with His grace.

"He giveth more grace" than all our need. It never runs short. Whatever our need is, there is quite enough grace for it, and then "more" too! *always* more. If our need seems to become greater, we shall find the grace greater too, if we will but go to Him who giveth it; if the enemies that we are trying to fight against seem stronger than ever, we shall certainly find His grace stronger too, if we will only ask it, and take it, and use it.

We can never overtake this promise, much less outrun it; for however little we have, or however much we want, now this moment, and on to the end of our lives, it is always, always, "He giveth *more* grace!"

"Have you on the Lord believed?
 Still there's more to follow;
Of His grace have you received?
 Still there's more to follow.
Oh the grace the Father shows!
 Still there's more to follow;
Freely He His grace bestows,
 Still there's more to follow.

"More and more! more and more!
 Always more to follow!
Oh His matchless, boundless love
 Still there's more to follow!"

26.

SATISFIED.

"Shall never thirst."—John iv. 14.

WHEN you have had a treat or a pleasure, do not you begin to wish for another? When you look over your playthings or your books (whichever you happen to care most for), have you not said, "If I only had just this, or just that besides"? And even some favored little ones who hardly know what to wish for, because they seem to have every thing, have not enough to make them *quite* happy; they want something, without knowing what they want. Is not this something like feeling thirsty?

And when you get the very thing you most wanted, it does not make much difference, for you very soon want something else; you are "thirsty" again.

The Lord Jesus knows all about this, and so He said, "Whosoever drinketh of this water shall thirst again; but whosoever drinketh of the water that I shall give him, shall never thirst." First, you see you are quite sure to "thirst again"; it is no use expecting to find any thing earthly that will satisfy you. Secondly, Jesus has something to give you which will make you *quite* satisfied and glad. Thirdly, as long as you go on drinking this, you will be *always* satisfied and glad. Fourthly, you can not get it from any one or any thing else. Jesus gives it, and Jesus only. Fifthly, it must be meant for you, because He says "whosoever," and that means "any body that likes!" And He says, "Ho, every one that thirsteth, come ye to the waters!" And, "If any man thirst, let him come unto me and drink." And, "I will give unto him that is athirst of the fountain of the water of life freely."

Will you not say to Him, like the poor woman at the well, "Lord Jesus, give me this water, that I thirst not!" Listen to his kind answer! "Drink, yea, drink abundantly, O beloved!"

"I heard the voice of Jesus say,
Behold, I freely give
The living water; thirsty one,
Stoop down, and drink, and live.

"I came to Jesus, and I drank
Of that life-giving stream;
My thirst was quenched, my soul revived,
And now I live in him."

27.

OUR SURETY.

"I will be surety for him."—GEN. xliii. 9.

JUDAH, the elder brother, promised his father to bring Benjamin safely back from Egypt. He undertook this entirely. He said, "I will be surety for him; of my hand shalt thou require him: if I bring him not unto thee, and set him before thee, then let me bear the blame forever." And his father trusted Judah to do as he had said, and so Judah was surety for Benjamin.

Jesus Christ is Surety for us. He, our Elder Brother, undertakes to bring us safely to the house of His Father and our Father. He undertakes to present us before the presence of His glory. We are in His hand, and from

His hand God will require us and receive us. And God, who so loves His children, has trusted the Lord Jesus to do this. He has given us to Him, and He has accepted Jesus Christ as our Surety.

Now, if God has trusted Him, will not you trust Him too? What! hesitate about trusting Jesus? Whom else could you trust? Who else could undertake to bring you safe to heaven? Benjamin might possibly have found his way by himself from Egypt to Canaan; but never, never could you find the way by yourself from earth to heaven; and never, never could any one but the Lord Jesus bring you there.

Benjamin could not be quite certain that his brother could keep his promise, for Judah was only a man, and might have been killed in Egypt. But you may be quite certain that your Elder Brother *can* keep His promise, for He is God as well as man. And do you think He *would* break His promise? He, the Faithful Saviour, break His promise? Heaven and earth shall pass away, but His word shall not pass away!

Then trust Him now, and never wrong His faithful love again by leaving off trusting Him. He is our Surety, and He will bring every one who trusts Him safe to the heavenly Canaan.

"Jesus, I will trust Thee, trust Thee with my soul!
Guilty, lost, and helpless, Thou canst make me whole!
Jesus, I do trust Thee, trust without a doubt!
'Whosoever cometh, Thou wilt not cast out.'"

28.

OUR FORERUNNER.

"He shall go over before."—DEUT. iii. 28.

JOSHUA was a type of Christ in many things. God gave him to be "a leader and commander of the people." He was their captain in war, and their saviour from their enemies.

In this verse God told Moses that Joshua should go over before the people into Canaan, and "cause them to inherit the land."

This is what the Lord Jesus Christ has done for us. He has gone before, in front of, the great army of the living God who have crossed or have yet to cross the river of death. His blessed feet have passed that river, and made the crossing easy for us, so that the dark waters shall never overflow one of us, not even a little child.

He has gone before us into the beautiful land to prepare the many mansions for us. He is there, waiting for us, ready to give us His own most sweet and gracious welcome to His own fair country, as soon as our feet have crossed the river.

Will you fear to go where Jesus has gone before? Will you fear to go where He is? You know you must die. You know that even little children die who are much younger than you. And very likely you do not like to think about dying. I do not think you need think at all about lying cold and dead and being put in the grave. When that does come, it will not matter to you in the least. If Jesus is your Saviour, if He takes away your sins, death will only be like being carried in a minute across a narrow stream, and meeting the loving and glorious

One on the other side, where He is gone over before. Nay, rather, He will come and fetch you Himself into the "pleasant land," and He will "cause you to inherit" it, so that it will be your own land, your own beautiful and holy and glorious home forever.

"Praying for His children,
In that blessed place,
Calling them to glory,
Sending them His grace;

"His bright home preparing,
Little ones, for you;
Jesus ever liveth,
Ever loveth too."

29.

"PLEASURES FOR EVERMORE."

"At Thy right hand there are pleasures for evermore."—Ps. xvi. 11.

YOU never had a pleasure that lasted. You look forward to a great pleasure, and it comes, and then very soon it is gone, and you can only look back upon it. The very longest and pleasantest day you ever had came to an end, and you had to go to bed and know that it was over.

How different are the pleasures at God's right hand! They are for evermore, and you can not get to the end or see to the end of "evermore," for there is no end to it.

And you see it is not one pleasure only, but "*pleasures,*" as manifold as they are unending. Do you not wonder what they will be? We can not even guess at most of them; and if we thought and imagined the brightest and best that we possibly could, we should still find, when we reached heaven, that God's "pleasures" for us were ever so much greater and better than we thought.

We can tell a few things about them. They will be holy pleasures, never mingled with any sin. They will be perfect pleasures, with nothing whatever to spoil them. They will be lasting pleasures, for to-night's text says so. They will be abundant pleasures, as many as we can possibly wish, for David says (Ps. xxxvi. 8), "They shall be *abundantly satisfied* with the fatness of Thy house, and Thou shalt make them drink of the river of Thy pleasures." They will be always freshly-flowing pleasures, for they are a river, not a little pool. They will be pleasures given by God Himself to us, for it does not say "they shall drink," but "*Thou* shalt *make them* drink of the river of *Thy* pleasures."

And all these "God hath prepared" for you. Is He not good and kind?

"Angel voices sweetly singing,
Echoes through the blue dome ringing,
News of wondrous gladness bringing,
Ah, 'tis heaven at last!

"Not a tear-drop ever falleth,
Not a pleasure ever palleth,
Song to song forever calleth;
Ah, 'tis heaven at last!"

30.

THE GREAT PROMISE.

"This is the promise that He hath promised us, even eternal life."—I JOHN ii. 25.

AS the gift of the Holy Spirit was specially "the promise of the Father," so it seems that the gift of eternal life was specially the promise of the Lord Jesus. If you look in the Gospel of St. John, you will find that He promised it not only once or twice, but fifteen times! So no wonder St. John in his Epistle calls it "*the* promise which He hath promised us."

If you made me a promise, even if you said it only once, you would expect me to believe it, would you not? And you would be vexed and hurt if I would not believe it. It would seem as if I thought you were not speaking the truth. And suppose I did not say whether I believed it or not, but simply took no notice at all of what you said, would not that be quite as bad?

Now when the Lord Jesus Himself has made us a great promise, does He not expect us to believe it? Surely it grieves Him more than any thing when we will not believe His kind words. And it seems almost worse when we do not take any notice of them, but go on just the same as if He had never promised any thing at all.

So you see it is not only that you *may* believe this great promise of the Lord Jesus, but that you *ought* to believe it, and that you are wronging His love and grieving His heart as long as you do not believe it.

No matter that you do not deserve it; that is true enough! but He has promised it!

No matter that it seems "too good

to be true"; for he has promised it! No matter that you don't feel as if you had got it yet,—He has promised it!

Only ask Him to give you faith like Abraham's, who was "fully persuaded that what He had promised He was able also to perform," so that you may say joyfully, "This is the promise that He hath promised *me*, even eternal life!"

"Life alone is found in Jesus,
Only there 'tis offered thee,
Offered without price or money,
'Tis the gift of God sent free.
Take salvation!
Take it now and happy be!"

31.

CERTAINTY.

"Hath He said, and shall He not do it!"
NUM. xxiii. 19.

WE have been thinking, night after night, of some of our Father's promises, and very likely you have been hoping and wishing that they would come true for you. But being quite sure is better and happier than hoping and wishing, is it not? Now, how may you be quite sure that all these "exceeding great and precious promises" will come true for you? Just simply because God has spoken them! and "hath He *said*, and shall He not do it?" Of course he will! Surely that is enough!

If your father had promised to give you a great treat, would you go about in a dismal way, saying, "Yes, it would be very nice? I hope papa will do it!" Would he be pleased at that? But if you came again, and reminded him of his promise, and he answered, "I have said it, and do you suppose I shall not do it?" what a silly child you would be if you still looked dismal, and went on only "hoping" he might do it! And what an ungrateful and unbelieving child you would be if you did not say brightly, "Thank you, dear papa!" and show him how glad you were about it, and try your very best to be good and please him all day, because he had made you such a kind and sure promise!

When you read the Bible, or hear it read; keep looking out for God's promises. They are scattered all over the Bible, like beautiful bright stars. Then, every time you come to one of them, say to yourself, This will come true for me, for "hath He said, and shall He not do it?"

Before you go to sleep, see if you can recollect as many promises as you are years old, and set upon every one this strong and shining seal, "Hath He said, and shall he not do it?"

When you reach the heavenly Canaan, you will find, as Joshua said, that "Not one thing hath failed of all the good things which the Lord your God spake concerning you; all are come to pass unto you, and not one thing hath failed thereof."—Josh. xxiii. 14.

"All that He hath spoken,
He will surely do!
Nothing shall be broken,
Every word is true."

MORNING BELLS;

OR,

WAKING THOUGHTS FOR THE LITTLE ONES.

BY

FRANCES RIDLEY HAVERGAL.

SOLID GROUND CHRISTIAN BOOKS
BIRMINGHAM, ALABAMA

CONTENTS.

MORNING BELLS.

MOST of the readers of this little book will have already read *Little Pillows.* Those were given you to go to sleep upon night after night; sweet, soothing texts, that little hearts might rest upon.

But in the morning we want something to arouse us, and to help us to go brightly and bravely through the day. So here are "Morning Bells" to waken up the little hearts, and to remind them that we must not only rest in Jesus, but walk in Him. If the motto of "Little Pillows" might be

"Come to Jesus," the motto of "Morning Bells" might be "Follow Jesus."

May He who loves the little ones bless this tiny effort to help them to follow Him day by day.

1.

First Day.

Christ's Childhood.

"Thy holy child Jesus."—ACTS iv. 30.

IF I asked, "How old are you?" you would give an exact answer. "Eight and a half;" "Just turned ten;" "Eleven next month." Now you have thought of God's "holy child Jesus" as a little baby, and as twelve years old in the temple, but did you ever think of Him as being *exactly* your own age? that He was once really just as old as you are this very day? He knows what it is to be eight, and nine, and ten years old, or whatever you may be. God's word has only told us this one thing about those years, that He was a *holy* child.

What is "holy"? It is everything that is perfectly beautiful and good and lovable, without anything to spoil it. This is just what He was when He was your age. He was gentle and brave, and considerate and unselfish, noble and truthful, obedient and loving, kind and forgiving,—everything you can think of that you ever admired or loved in any one else was all found together in Him, and all this not only outside, but inside, for He was "holy."

Why did He live all these holy child-years on earth instead of staying in heaven till it was time to come and die for you? One reason was, that He might leave you a beautiful example, so that you might wish to be like Him, and ask for the Holy Spirit to make you like Him. But the other was even more gracious and wonderful, it was "that we might be made the righteousness of God in Him." That is, that all this goodness and holiness might be reckoned to you, because you had not any of your own, and that God might smile on you *for His sake*, just as if *you* had been perfectly obedient, and truthful, and unselfish, and good, and give you Jesus Christ's reward, which you never deserved at all, but which He deserved for you.

He took your sins and gives you His righteousness; He took your punishment and gives you His reward; it is just changed over, if you will only accept the exchange!

"I'm glad my blessed Saviour
 Was once a child like me,
To show how pure and holy
 His little ones might be.
And if I try to follow
 His footsteps here below,
He never will forget me,
 Because He loves me so."

2.

Second Day.

Our Great Example.

"Even Christ pleased not Himself."—
ROM. xv. 3.

DO you really wish to follow the footsteps of the Holy Child Jesus? Have you asked God to make you more like Him? Are you ready to begin to-day? Then here is a motto for to-day, "Even Christ pleased not Himself." Will you take it, and try to imitate Him? You are sure to have plenty of opportunities of acting upon it, and thus proving not only to others, but to your dear Saviour Himself, that you mean what you say, and mean what you pray.

Perhaps it seems a rather melancholy

"morning bell" to you, tolling instead of chiming! But if you really wish to be like Christ, you will soon find that its music is as sweet as any, and that its quiet chime will come to you again and again with a wonderful sweetness and power, helping you over all sorts of difficulties, and saving you from all sorts of sins and troubles.

You can not tell, till you have fairly tried, how happy a little girl can feel, who has cheerfully given up to another, for Jesus' sake, something which she would have liked for herself; nor how happy a boy can be when of his own free will, and by God's grace, he has chosen to do what his conscience tells him would please the Lord Jesus instead of what would have pleased himself.

If you have never tried it yet, begin to-day, and you will find it is quite a new happiness.

Ah, what would have become of us if Christ had only "pleased Himself," and had stayed in His own glorious home instead of coming down to save us! Think of that when you are tempted to please yourself instead of pleasing Him, and the remembrance that even He pleased not Himself because He so loved you, will help you to try and please Him, and to please others for His sake.

"If washed in Jesus' blood,
Then bear His likeness too!
And as you onward press,
Ask, 'What would Jesus do?'

"Give with a full, free hand;
God freely gives to you!
And check each selfish thought
With, 'What would Jesus do?'"

3.

Third Day.

Upholding.

"Hold Thou me up, and I shall be safe."—
Ps. cxix. 117.

THE path is not easy. There are rough stones over which we may stumble, if we are not walking very carefully. There are places which look quite smooth, but they are more dangerous than the rough ones, for they are slippery. There are little holes hidden under flowers, which may catch our feet and give us a bad fall. There are muddy ditches, into which we may slip and get sadly wet and dirty.

How are we to walk safely along such a path? We want a strong, kind hand to hold us up, and to hold us always; a hand that will hold ours so tightly and lovingly, that it will be as the old Scotchwoman said, "Not my grip of Christ, but Christ's grip of me!" Yes, Christ's loving hand is "able to keep you from falling;" only "let your hand be restfully in the hand of Jesus," and "then shalt thou walk in thy way safely, and thy foot shall not stumble."

But do not spoil the chime of this morning's bells by ringing only half a peal! Do not say, "Hold Thou me up," and stop there, or add, "But, all the same, I shall stumble and fall!" Finish the peal with God's own music, the bright words of faith that He puts into your mouth, "Hold Thou me up, *and I shall be safe!*" So you will if you do not distrust Him, if you will but *trust* Him to do just what you ask, and let Him hold you up.

It would be hard to find a prayer in the Bible without a promise to match it; so David says, "Uphold me, according to Thy word."

What has He said about it? More than there is room for on this page. "I the Lord thy God will hold thy right hand." "Yea, I will uphold thee." "He will not suffer thy foot to be moved." "When thou runnest thou shalt not stumble." "Yea, he shall be holden up." "He shall keep thy foot from being taken." "He will keep the feet of His saints." Seven promises in answer to your one little prayer!

"I the Lord am with thee,
Be thou not afraid!
I will help and strengthen,
Be thou not dismayed!
Yea, I will uphold thee
With my own right hand;
Thou art called and chosen
In my sight to stand."

4.

Fourth Day.

What can I do?

"Bear ye one another's burdens, and so fulfill the law of Christ."—GAL. vi. 2.

PERHAPS you never thought that any one around you had any! Then if you want to fulfill this law of Christ, the first thing will be to find out who has any burdens, and which of them you could bear instead. You will not have to watch long! There are very few without any. Little backs can not bear great burdens, but sometimes those who have great burdens have little ones too, and it makes such a difference if some loving little hand will take one or two of these. If your mother was carrying a great heavy parcel, would it not help her if you took two or three little ones out of her hand and carried them for her? So perhaps she has troubles that you do not even know about, and you see she looks tired and anxious. And it tires her a little more, because a little brother or sister wants to be nursed or amused. Now if you put your own affairs by, and call the little ones away, and amuse them quietly so that mamma may not be disturbed, this is bearing one of her burdens. Never mind if it is really a little burden to you too; is it not worth it, when it is fulfilling the law of Christ? If for a moment a burden that you have taken up does seem rather hard, and you are tempted to drop it again, think of what the Lord Jesus bore for you! Think how He took up the heaviest burden of all for you, when He "His own self bare our sins in His own body on the tree!" He did not drop that burden, but bore it till He died under it. Think of that, and it will be easy then to bear something for His sake.

Now be on the watch all to-day for little burdens to bear for others. See how many you can find out, and pick up, and carry away! Depend upon it, you will not only make it a brighter day for others, but for yourself too!

" Little deeds of kindness,
Little words of love,
Make our earth an Eden,
Like the heaven above.'

5.

Fifth Day.

Instruments.

"Yield . . . . your members as instruments of righteousness unto God."—ROM. vi. 13.

THIS does not sound so easy and tuneful as most of your other "morning bells," you think! But listen for a few minutes and you will hear the music.

What are your members? Hands, feet, lips, eyes, ears, and so on. What are you to do with them? "Yield" them, that is, give them up altogether, hand them over to God.

What for? That He may use them as instruments of righteousness. That is, just as we should take an instrument of music, to make music with it, so He may take your hands and feet and all your members, and use them to do right and good things with.

If a little one gives himself or herself to God, every part of that little body is to be God's little servant, a little instrument for Him to use.

The little hands will no longer serve Satan by striking or pinching; the little feet will not kick or stamp, nor drag and dawdle, when they ought to run briskly on some errand; the little lips will not pout; the little tongue will not move to say a naughty thing. All the little members will leave off serving Satan, and find something to do for God; for if you "yield" them to God, He will really take them and use them.

He will tell the hands to pick up what a tired mamma has dropped, and to fetch her a footstool; and the fingers to sew patiently at a warm petticoat for a poor child, or to make warm cuffs for a poor old man. He will tell the feet to run on errands of kindness and help. He will set the lips to sing happy hymns, which will cheer and comfort somebody, even if you never know of it. He will use the eyes for reading to some poor sick or blind woman, or to some fretful little one in your own home. You will be quite surprised to find in how many ways He will really use even your little members, if you give them and your whole self to Him. It will be so nice! You will never be miserable again with "nothing to do!"

"Take my hands, and let them move
At the impulse of Thy love.
Take my feet, and let them be
Swift and 'beautiful' for Thee."

6.

Sixth Day.

Willing and Glad.

"Then the people rejoiced, for that they offered willingly."—1 CHRON. xxix. 9

WE thought yesterday morning about giving our members up to God for Him to use. Did you think you would like to give them up to Him? *did* you yield them to Him? If you did, you will understand this morning's text! David the King asked his people to help in bringing offerings for God's house and service. He said, "Who then is willing to consecrate his service this day unto the Lord?" And God made them all willing to bring what they could. And what then? "*Then* the people rejoiced, for that they offered willingly, because with perfect heart they offered willingly to the Lord." "And did eat and drink on that day before the Lord with great gladness."

See what came of offering willingly to the Lord—they "rejoiced," and everything they did, even eating and drinking, was "with great gladness." Never is any one so happy as those who offer their own selves willingly to the Lord. He gives them a thousandfold return for the worthless little self and weak little members which they have offered to Him. He gives them peace, and gladness, and blessing, beyond what they ever expected to have.

But this was not all; it was not only the people who had such a glad day, but "David the king also rejoiced with great joy." Those who loved their king, and recollected how much sorrow he had gone through, and how many battles he had fought for them, must have been glad indeed to see Him rejoicing because they had offered willingly. And I think our King, *your* King Jesus, rejoices over us when He has made us able (ver. 14) to offer ourselves willingly to Him. Is not this best of all? Jesus, who suffered for us, and who fought the great battle of our salvation for us, He, our own beloved King, "will rejoice over thee with joy; He will rest in His love; He will joy over thee with singing."

"In full and glad surrender I give myself to
Thee,
Thine utterly, and only, and evermore to be!
O Son of God, who lovest me, I will be
Thine alone;
And all I have, and all I am, shall henceforth be Thine own."

7.

Seventh Day.

Faithfulness.

"Faithful over a few things."—MATT. XXV. 21, 23.

THE servant who had only two talents to trade with, but traded faithfully with them, had just the same glorious words spoken to him as the servant who had five talents: "Well done, good and faithful servant: thou hast been faithful over a few things . . . . enter thou into the joy of thy lord." Think what it would be to hear the Lord Jesus saying that to you, really to you! Oh how sweet! how blessed! how you would listen to that gracious voice saying those wonderfully gracious words to *you!*

But could He say them to you?

Are you "faithful over a few things"? He has given every one, even the youngest, a few things to be faithful over, and so He has to you. Your "few things" may be very few, and very small things, but He expects you to be faithful over them.

What is being faithful over them? It means doing the very best you can with them; doing as much for Jesus as you can with your money, even if you have very little; doing as much for Him as you can with your time; doing whatever duties He gives you as well as ever you can,—your lessons, your work, the little things that you are bidden or asked to do every day, the little things that you have promised or undertaken to do for others. It means doing all these just the same whether others see you or know about it or not.

You sigh over all this; you recollect many things in which you have not been quite faithful; you know you do not deserve for Him to call you "good and faithful servant." But come at once to your gracious Lord, and ask Him to forgive all the unfaithfulness, and to make you faithful to-day. And then, even if it is only a matter of a French verb or a Latin noun, you will find it a help to recollect, "Faithful over a few things!"

"Only, O Lord, in Thy dear love
Fit us for perfect rest above;
And help us, this and every day,
To live more nearly as we pray."

8.

Eighth Day.

"On mine Account."

" Put that on mine account."—PHILEM. 18.

WHEN St. Paul asked Philemon, in a most beautiful letter, to take back Onesimus, who had run away from him, he said, " If he hath wronged thee, or oweth thee ought, put that on my account." Onesimus had been a bad servant to Philemon; and being willing to come back and do better, would not pay for what he had wronged him in before, and would not pay his old debts. And he evidently had nothing himself to pay them with. But St. Paul offered to pay all, so that Onesimus might be received, " not now as a servant," but as a "brother beloved."

This is an exquisite picture of what the Lord Jesus Christ does. He not only intercedes for us with Him from whom we have departed, and against whom we have sinned; but, knowing to the full how much we have wronged God, and how much we owe Him, He says, "Put that on mine account."

And God has put it all on His account, and the account has been paid, paid in blood. When "the Lord laid on Him the iniquity of us all," Jesus saw and knew all your sins; and He said, "Put that on mine account."

Oh, what wonderful "kindness and love of God our Saviour!" Let the remembrance of it be like a silver bell, ringing softly and clearly whenever you are going to do, or letting yourself feel or think, something that is not right.

"Put *that* on mine account!" Yes, that sin that you were on the very edge of committing! that angry word, and the angry feeling that makes you want to say it; that untrue word, and the cowardliness which makes you afraid to speak the exact truth; that proud look, and the naughty pride of heart that made it come into your eyes; Jesus stands by and says, patiently and lovingly, "Put *that* on mine account!"

Can you bear that? does it not make you wish, ten times more than ever, to be kept from sinning against such a Saviour?

"Jesus, tender Saviour,
  Hast Thou died for me?
Make me very thankful
  In my heart to Thee;
When the sad, sad story
  Of Thy grief I read,
Make me very sorry
  For my sins indeed."

9.

Ninth Day.

White Garments.

"Let thy garments be always white."—
ECCLES. ix. 8.

"ALWAYS?" Oh, how can that be? They are soiled again directly after they have been washed clean! Yet God says, "Let them be *always* white;" and He would not tell you to do what was impossible. Then how are you to help soiling them? Only in one way. Last night's "little pillow" told you how Jesus washes us "whiter than snow" in His own precious blood, that cleanseth from all sin. But will He only cleanse His little one just for the moment? is that all He is able and willing to do for you?

No; if you will only keep on trusting to that precious blood, and not turn away from it, He says that it cleanseth, that is, *goes on cleansing*. You could not keep your garments white for five minutes; careless thoughts would come like dust upon them, and wrong words would make great dark stains, and before long some naughty deed would be like a sad fall in the mud, and you would feel sad and ashamed before the kind Saviour who still stands ready to cleanse you again. But why should all this happen over and over again, till anybody but our own loving, long-suffering Saviour would be tired of us, and give up doing any more for us? Why should it be, when His precious blood is meant to "*go on cleansing*," so that our garments may be always white? Perhaps you never thought of this; ask

Him now this morning not only to wash you in the fountain of His precious blood, but *to keep you in it*, to *go on cleansing* you all day long. *Trust* Him to do this, and see if it is not the happiest day you ever spent!

"And He can do all this for me,
Because in sorrow, on the tree,
He once for sinners hung;
And, having washed their sin away,
He now rejoices, day by day,
To cleanse His little one."

10.

Tenth Day.

Made Beautiful.

"Let the beauty of the Lord our God be upon us."—Ps. xc. 17.

"HOW great is His beauty!" said Zechariah. How can His beauty be upon us? In two ways; try to understand them, and then ask that in both ways the beauty of the Lord our God may be upon you.

One way is by His covering you with the robe of Jesus Christ's righteousness, looking upon you not as you are in yourself, all sinful and unholy, but as if all the Saviour's beautiful and holy life were yours, reckoning it to you for His sake. In this way He can call us "perfect through my comeliness which I had put upon thee." The other way is by giving you the beauty of holiness, for that is His own beauty; and though we never can be quite like Him till we see Him as He is, He can begin to make us like Him even now. Look at a poor little colorless drop of water, hanging weakly on a blade of grass. It is not beautiful at all; why should you stop to look at it? Stay till the sun has risen, and now look. It is sparkling like a diamond; and if you look at it from another side, it will be glowing like a ruby, and presently gleaming like an emerald. The poor little drop has become one of the brightest and loveliest things you ever saw. But is it its own brightness and beauty? No; if it slipped down to the ground out of the sunshine, it would be only a poor little dirty drop of water. So, if the Sun of Righteousness, the glorious and lovely Saviour, shines upon you, a little ray of His own brightness and beauty will be seen upon you. Sometimes we can see by the happy light on a face that the Sun is shining there; but if the Sun is really shining, there are sure to be some of the beautiful rays of holiness, love, joy, peace, gentleness, goodness, faith, meekness, making the life even of a little child very lovely.

"Jesus, Lord, I come to Thee,
Thou hast said I may;
Tell me what my life should be,
Take my sins away.

"Jesus, Lord, I learn of Thee,
In Thy word divine;
Every promise there I see,
May I call it mine!"

II.

Eleventh Day.

Pleasant Gifts.

"Who giveth us richly all things to enjoy." —I TIM. vi. 17.

THINK a little this morning of God's great kindness to you. How *very* good He is to you! I know one of His dear children who looks up many, many times a day, and says, "*Good* Lord Jesus!" or "*Kind* Lord Jesus!" She does not set herself to say it, but it seems as if she could not help saying it, just because He *is* so good and kind. And then it seems only natural to look up again and say, "*Dear* Lord Jesus!" How *can* anybody go on all day long, and never see how good He is, and never look up and bless Him? Most especially on bright pleasant days, when He giveth us more even than usual to enjoy! "He giveth." Not one single pleasant thing, not one single bit of enjoyment comes to us but what He giveth. We can not get it, we do not earn it, we do not deserve it; but He *giveth* lovingly, and kindly, and freely. Suppose He stopped giving, what would become of us?

"Richly." So richly, that if you tried to write down half His gifts to you, your hand would be tired long before you had done. You might easily make a list of the presents given you on your birthday, but you could not make a list of what God gives you every day of your life.

"All things." All the things you really need, and a great many more besides. All the things that will do you good, a great many more than you would ever have thought of. All the things that He can fill your little hands with, and trust you to carry without stumbling and falling. *All* things, everything that you have at all!

"To enjoy." Now how kind this is! not only "to do us good," but "to enjoy." So you see He means you to be happy with what He gives you, to smile and laugh and be glad, not to be dismal and melancholy. If you do not enjoy what He "giveth," that is your own fault, for He meant you to enjoy it. Look up to Him with a bright smile, and thank Him for having given you richly all things to enjoy!

"My joys to Thee I bring,
The joys Thy love hath given,
That each may be a wing
To lift me nearer heaven.
I bring them, Saviour, all to Thee,
For Thou hast purchased all for me."

12.

Twelfth Day.

Much more than this.

"The Lord is able to give thee much more than this."—2 CHRON. xxv. 9.

AMAZIAH, king of Judah, was going to war against the Edomites. He thought he would make sure of victory by hiring a hundred thousand soldiers from the King of Israel, and he paid them beforehand a hundred talents, which was about £34,218. 15s. of our money. But a man of God warned him not to let the army of Israel go with him, for Israel had forsaken the Lord, and so He was not with them. It seemed a great pity to waste all that money, and so Amaziah said, "But what shall we do for the hundred talents which I have given to the army of Israel? And the man of God answered, The Lord is able to give thee much more than this." So Amaziah simply obeyed, and sent the soldiers away, and trusted God to help him to do without them. Was it any wonder that he gained a great victory over the Edomites?

Does not this teach us that we should simply do the right thing, and trust God at any cost? When you do this, you will find that, in hundreds of ways which you never thought of, "the Lord is able to give thee much more." The trial comes in many different ways. One may be tempted to hurry over prayer and Bible, because there is something else that she very much wants to get done before breakfast, and she is afraid of not having time enough. Another shuts up her little purse when a call comes to give something for God's work, because she is afraid she will not have enough left for another purpose. Another is tempted to look at a key, or to glance over another's shoulder at a lesson, because without it he would not get the marks he is trying for Another is tempted not to tell the exact truth, or to conceal something which he ought to tell, because he would lose something by it. Oh, resist the devil, and do what you know is right, and trust God for all the rest! For "the Lord is able to give thee much more than this," whatever your "*this*" may be. And His smile and His blessing will always be "more than this," more than anything else!

"Be brave to do the right,
  And scorn to be untrue;
When fear would whisper 'yield!'
  Ask, 'What would Jesus do?'"

Thirteenth Day.

13.

The Doings of the King.

"Whatsoever the king did pleased all the people."—2 SAM. iii. 36.

DAVID had been giving a proof of his love for one who had long been his enemy, but whom he had received into friendship; and he had been giving a proof of his tender-heartedness and sympathy with the people, by weeping with them at the grave of Abner. "And all the people took notice of it, and it pleased them: as whatsoever the king did pleased all the people."

This was because they loved their king. They watched him, not as the wicked Pharisees watched the Lord

Jesus that they might find something against Him; but with the watching of admiration and love, taking notice of the kind and gracious things he did and said. Do you thus take notice of what your King does? Does it please you to hear and read of what He has done and what He is doing? It must be so if He really is your King.

But the "whatsoever" is a little harder; and yet, if it is once really learnt, it makes everything easy. For if we learn to be pleased with *whatsoever* our King Jesus does, nothing can come wrong to us.

Suppose something comes to-day which is not quite what you would have liked; heavy rain, for instance, when you wanted to go out,—recollect that your King Jesus has done it, and that will hush the little murmur, and make you quite content. Ask Him this morning to make you so loving and loyal to Him, that *whatsoever* He does, all day long, may please you, because it has pleased Him to do it. I think He loves us so much, that He always gives us as much happiness as He can possibly trust us with, and does what is pleasantest for His dear children whenever He sees it will not hurt them; so, when He does something which at first does not seem so pleasant, we may still trust our beloved King, and learn by His grace to be pleased with *whatsoever* He does.

"I hear a sweet voice ringing clear,
'All is well!'
It is my Father's voice I hear,
All is well!
Where'er I walk that voice is heard,
It is my God, my Father's word—
'Fear not, but trust; I am the Lord,
All is well!'"

14.

Fourteenth Day.

The New Heart.

"A new heart also will I give you."—
EZEK. xxxvi. 26.

WHY does God promise this? Because our old hearts are so evil that they can not be made any better; and so nothing will do any good but giving us a quite new heart.

Because we can not make a new heart for ourselves; the more we try, the more we shall find we can not do it; so God, in His great pity and kindness, says He will give it us.

Because unless we have a new heart we can not enter the kingdom of God, we can not even see it! Without this gift we must be left outside in the terrible darkness when "the door is shut."

What is the difference? The old heart *likes* to be naughty in some way or other; either it likes to be idle, or it likes to let out sharp words, or to go on being sulky or fretful instead of clearing up and saying. "I am sorry!" The new heart *wants* to be good; and is grieved when a temptation comes, and does not wish to yield to it; and would like to be always pleasing the Saviour.

The old heart is afraid of God, and does not love Him, and would much rather He were not always seeing us. And it does not care to hear about Jesus, but would rather be just let alone. The new heart loves God and trusts what He says, and likes to know that He is always watching it. And it is glad to hear about Jesus, and wants to come closer to Him.

The old heart is a little slave of Satan, taking his orders, and doing what he wishes. The new heart is a happy little servant of Christ, listening to His orders, and doing what He wishes.

Oh how happy and blessed to have this new heart! All God's own children receive it, for He has said, "I will give them one heart;" that is, all the same new heart. Do you not want to have it too? Then "ask, and you *shall* receive;" for He hath said, "A new heart also *will* I give you!"

"Oh for a heart to praise my God,
  A heart from sin set free!
A heart that always feels Thy blood,
  So freely shed for me.

"A heart resigned, submissive, meek,
  My dear Redeemer's throne;
Where only Christ is heard to speak,
  Where Jesus reigns alone."

Fifteenth Day.

15.

The Gift of the Holy Spirit.

"I will put my Spirit within you."—
EZEK. xxxvi. 27.

MANY years ago a good clergyman wrote a tiny prayer, so short that no one could help remembering it if they once heard it. God seemed to set that little prayer "upon wheels," so that it might run everywhere. It was printed on large cards and hung up, and it was printed on small ones and kept in Bibles and pocket-books. It was taught to classes and schools and whole congregations, and now thousands upon thousands pray it constantly. It is a prayer which must be heard, because it asks for what God has promised to give; and it asks for this through Him whom the Father heareth always. It is this: "O God, give me Thy Holy Spirit, for Jesus Christ's sake. Amen." Will you not pray it too? Begin this morning, and go on, not just *saying* it, but *praying* it, till you get a full answer. For you are quite sure to get it; here is God's own promise, "I *will* put my Spirit within you;" and He has promised it over and over again in other places. Perhaps you will not know at first when the answer comes. Can you see the dew fall? No one ever saw a single drop come down, and yet as soon as the sun rises, you see that it has come, and is sparkling all over the fields. It came long before you saw it, falling sweetly and silently in the twilight and in the dark. So do not fancy God is not hearing you because you have not felt anything very sudden and wonderful. He is hearing and answering all the time. You would not go on asking unless the dew of His Spirit were already falling upon your heart, and teaching you to pray. The more He gives you of His blessed Spirit, the more you will ask for; and the more you ask, the more He will give.

"Thou gift of Jesus, now descend,
And be my Comforter and Friend;
O Holy Spirit, fill my heart,
That I from Christ may ne'er depart!

"Show me my soul all black within,
And cleanse and keep me pure within;
Oh, show me Jesus! let me rest
My heart upon His loving breast!"

16.

Sixteenth Day.

How to Conquer.

"The Lord shall fight for you."—Ex. xiv. 14.

HOW glad the children of Israel must have been when Moses said these words to them on the shores of the Red Sea! For when they "lifted up their eyes, behold, the Egyptians marched after them; and they were sore afraid."

The Egyptians had been cruel masters to them; and they had horses and chariots to pursue them with; and there was the sea close before them, and no boats! Perhaps some of the Israelites thought it was no use trying to escape, they would only be overtaken and conquered, and be worse off than before.

And so, left to themselves, they would have been; but God fought for them in a way they never thought of. For "the Lord saved Israel that day out of the hand of the Egyptians, and Israel saw the Egyptians dead upon the sea-shore."

What about your Egyptians?—the angry tempers or sulky looks, the impatient words, the vain and foolish thoughts, the besetting sins that master you so often. Have you tried so often to fight against them, and failed, that it seems almost no use, and you do not see how to conquer them or to escape them? Are you very tired of fighting, and "sore afraid" of being always overcome just the same as ever? Now hear God's true, strong promise to you. "The Lord shall fight for you!" "Will He really?" Yes, really, and He will conquer for you too, if you will only believe His Word and trust the battle to Him, and *let* Him fight for you.

How? First, watch! and then the very instant you see the enemy coming, look up and say, "Come, Lord, and fight for me;" and keep on looking up and *expecting* Him to fight for you. And *you will find* that He does fight for you and gives you the victory; and you too will be "saved that day," and will see "the Egyptians dead upon the sea-shore." Try Him, and trust Him; and you, even you, will be "more than conqueror through Him that loved you."

"So, when you meet with trials,
  And know not what to do;
Just cast the care on Jesus,
  And He will fight for you.
Gird on the heavenly armor
  Of faith, and hope, and love;
And when the conflict's ended,
  You'll reign with Him above."

Seventeenth Day.

17.

The Master's Voice.

"I will watch to see what He will say unto me."—HAB. ii. 1.

WHEN the Lord Jesus said to Simon the Pharisee, "Simon, I have somewhat to say unto thee;" he answered, "Master, say on!" When God was going to speak to Samuel, he said, "Speak, Lord, for Thy servant heareth." Has the Lord Jesus said anything like this for us? He says, "I have yet many things to say unto you." What things? They will be strong, helpful, life-giving words, for He says, "The words that I speak unto you, they are spirit and they are life." They will be very loving words, for He says, "I will speak comfortably to her" (margin, "I will speak to her heart"). And they will be very kind and tender words, and spoken just at the right moment, for He says that He knows "how to speak a word in season to him that is weary." "Will He really speak to me?" says the little heart. Yes, really, if you will only watch to see what He will say to you. For it will be "a still, small voice," and you will not hear it at all if you do not listen for it. "How will He speak to me?" If I had something very nice to tell you, and instead of saying it out loud, I wrote it down on a piece of paper, and gave it you to look at, would not that be exactly the same as if I had told it you with my lips? And you would take the paper eagerly to see what it was that I had to say to you. So to-day, when you read your Bible, either alone or at your

Bible-lesson, watch to see what Jesus will say to you in it. You will never really watch in vain. You will see some word that seems to come home to you, and that you never noticed so much before. Oh, listen lovingly to it, for *that* is what He says to you! Or if you are really watching and wishing for a word from Him, some sweet text will come into your mind, and you wonder what made you think of it! That is the voice of Jesus speaking to your heart. Listen to it, and treasure it up, and follow it; and then watch to see what else He will say to you. Say to Him, "Master, say on!"

"Master, speak! and make me ready,
  When Thy voice is truly heard,
With obedience glad and steady,
  Still to follow every word.
I am listening, Lord, for Thee;
Master, speak, oh, speak to me!"

Eighteenth Day.

18.

Who will take care of me?

"He careth for you."—1 PET. v. 7.

IT is so pleasant to be cared for; to have kind relations and friends who show that they love you by their care of you, and their care for you. What would you do if no one cared for you, like the poor little children in London who are turned out to "do for themselves" before they are as old as you are? What would you do if there was no one to get anything for you to eat, or to see to your clothes, or to keep a home for you to live in? No one to take any notice if you hurt yourself ever so badly, or if you were ever so ill? You would feel then what a difference being cared for makes to your life. But all the earthly care for you comes because "He careth for you." He planned and arranged everything, without your having anything to do with it, so that you shall be cared for. And He did not arrange it once for all, and then leave things to go on as might happen. No! Every day, every moment, He careth, *goes on* caring, for you. Not only thinking of you and watching you, but working for you; making things come right, so that everything should be just the best that could happen to you. Not managing the great things, and leaving the little things to arrange themselves; but giving loving care to the least, the very least things that concern you. Even in some tiny little trouble which no one else seems to care about, "He careth;" or when every one else is too much taken up with other things to attend to you, "He careth for you."

You can never get beyond God's care, for it always reaches you; you can never be outside of it, for it is always enfolding you.

"'Who will take care of me?' darling, you say,
Lovingly, tenderly watched as you are?
Listen! I give you the answer to-day,
ONE who is never forgetful or far.

"He will take care of you! All through the year
Crowning each day with His kindness and love,
Sending you blessings and shielding from fear,
Leading you on to His bright home above."

Nineteenth Day.

19.

Under His Wings.

"Under His wings shalt thou trust."—
Ps. xci. 4.

THAT means to-day, not some other time! Under His wings, the shadowing wings of the Most High, you, poor little helpless one, are to trust to-day.

When the little eaglets, that have not yet a feather to fly with, are under the great wings of the parent eagle, how safe they are! Who would dare touch them? If a bold climber put his hand into the nest then, those powerful wings would beat him in a minute from his hold, and he would fall down the rocks and be dashed to pieces. So safe shall you be "under

His wings," "nothing shall by any means hurt you" there.

When the wild snow-storms rage round the eyrie, and the mountain cold is felt, that is death to an unprotected sleeper, how warm the little eaglets are kept! Not an arrow of the keen blast reaches them, poor little featherless things, not a snowflake touches them. So warm shall you be kept "under His wings," when any cold and dark day of trouble comes, or even any sudden little blast of unkindness or loneliness.

"Under His wings shalt thou *trust!*" Not "shalt thou *see!*" If one of the eaglets wanted to see for itself what was going on, and thought it could take care of itself for a little while, and hopped from under the shadow of the wings, it would be neither safe nor warm. The sharp wind would chill it, and the cruel hand might seize it then.

So you are to *trust*, rest quietly and peacefully, "under His wings;" stay there, not be peeping out and wondering whether God really is taking care of you! You may be always safe and happy there. Safe, for "in the shadow of Thy wings will I make my refuge." Happy, for "in the shadow of Thy wings will I rejoice."

Remember, too, that it is a command as well as a promise; it is what you are to do to-day, all day long: "Under His wings *shalt* thou trust!"

"I am trusting Thee, Lord Jesus,
Trusting only Thee!
Trusting Thee for full salvation,
Great and free.

"I am trusting Thee to guide me,
Thou alone shalt lead!
Every day and hour supplying
All my need."

20.

Twentieth Day.

Always Near.

"I am with you alway."—MATT. xxviii. 20.

HOW nice it would be if we could always have the one we loved best in all the world with us; never away from us night or day, and no fear that they ever possibly would or could leave us; never a good-bye even for ever such a little while, and never, never the long farewell of death!

Can this ever be for you? Yes, for you; for to every one who is a disciple of the Lord Jesus (that is, who learns of Him and owns Him as Master), He says, "I am with you alway." He does not even say, "I will be with you;" so that you might be wondering when He meant to come, when He would begin to be "with you;" but He says, "I *am* with you." Yes, even now, though perhaps your eyes are holden, like those of the two who walked to Emmaus, when Jesus was beside them and they did not know it. Your feeling or not feeling that He is there has nothing at all to do with it, because His word must be true and *is* true, and He has said, "I *am* with you alway." All you have to do is to be happy in believing it to be true. And if you go on believing it, you will soon begin to realize it; that is, to find that it is a real thing, and that Jesus really is with you.

How long will He be with you? Always, "all the days!" He hath said, "I will never leave thee." "Never" means really *never*, not for one moment. You can not get beyond "never." It goes on all through your life, and all through God's great "forever." And "always" means really *always*, every single moment of all your life, so that you need never ask again, "Is Jesus with me now?" Of course He is! the answer will always be "yes," because He hath said, "I am with you alway." How safe, how sweet, how blessed!

"O Jesus, make Thyself to me
A living, bright reality!
More present to faith's vision keen
Than any outward object seen;
More dear, more intimately nigh,
Than even the sweetest earthly tie."

Twenty-first Day.

21.

Doing God's Will.

"Teach me to do Thy will."—Ps. cxliii. 10.

WHEN you see some one doing with very great delight some beautiful and pleasant piece of work, have you not thought, "I should like to be able to do that!" and perhaps you have said, "Please, teach me how to do it."

Can you think of anything pleasanter to do than what the very angels are full of delight in doing? Can you think of anything more beautiful to do than what is done in the "pleasant land," the beautiful home above? Can you fancy anything more interesting to do than what the dwellers there will never get tired of doing for thousands of millions of years? Would you not like to be taught to do it too?—to begin the pleasant and beautiful and most interesting work now, instead of waiting till you are grown up, and then perhaps never learning it at all, because it was put off now? Then pray this little prayer this morning with all your heart, "Teach me to do Thy will." For it is His will that is the happiest work above, and the very happiest thing to do here below.

What is His will? The Prayer-Book version of this Psalm tells you very simply and sweetly. It says, "Teach me to do the thing that pleaseth Thee." So doing God's will is just doing the things, one by one, that please Him.

Why did David ask this? He goes on to say why—"For Thou art my God." If God is really *our* God, we too shall wish to do the thing that pleaseth Him. David did not think he could do it of himself, for he says next, "Let Thy loving Spirit lead me." That loving Spirit will lead you too, dear child, and show you how beautiful and grand God's will is, and make you long to do it always, and teach you to do it. So that even on earth you may begin to do what the angels are doing in heaven!

"It is but very little
For Him that I can do,
Then let me seek to serve Him,
My earthly journey through;
And, without sigh or murmur,
To do His holy will;
And in my daily duties
His wise commands fulfill."

Twenty-second Day.

22.

Working for Jesus.

"Ye have done it unto me." "Ye did it not to me."—MATT. xxv., xl., and xlv.

OUR Lord Jesus Christ has given us opportunities of showing whether we love Him or not. He tells us that what we try to do for any one who is poor, or hungry, or sick, or a lonely stranger, is just the same as doing it to Him. And when the King says, "Come, ye blessed," He will remember these little things, and will say, "Ye have done it unto me." But He tells us that if we do nothing for them, it is just the same as if He were standing there and we would do nothing for Him. And He will say, "Ye did it not to me."

One of these two words will be spoken to you in the great day when you see the King on the throne of His glory. Which shall it be? What are you doing for Jesus? Are you doing anything at all for Him? Perhaps you say, "I have no opportunity." Did you ever try to find one? Did you ever ask Him to give you opportunities of doing something for Him? Or is it only that you have never yet cared or tried to do anything for Him? Be honest about it. He knows. And He will forgive.

But now, what is to be done? Begin by asking Him to show you. And then keep a bright, sharp look-out, and see if you can not find an opportunity very soon (and perhaps many) of doing something kind for His sake to some poor or sick or lonely one. Set to work to *think* what you could do!

It seems to me so very kind of the Lord Jesus to have told us this. For He knew that those who really love Him would *want* to do something for Him, and what could we do for the King of glory in His glorious heaven? So it was wonderfully thoughtful of Him to give us His poor people to care for, and to say, if we have only been kind to a sick old woman or hungry little child, "Ye have done it unto me!"

> "I love my precious Saviour
> Because He died for me;
> And if I did not serve Him,
> How sinful I should be!
> God help me to be useful
> In all I do or say!
> I mean to work for Jesus,
> The Bible says I may!'"

Twenty-third Day.

23.

Standard-Bearers.

"Thou hast given a banner to them that fear Thee."—Ps. lx. 4.

THEN what is your banner, and what are you doing with it? For if you are among "them that fear" God, He has given you a banner "that it may be displayed." Is yours furled up and put away in a corner, so that nobody sees it or knows of it? Or are you trying to be a brave little standard-bearer of Jesus Christ, carrying His flag, so that the sweet breezes of His Spirit may lift its bright folds, and show its golden motto? That motto, I think, is "Love." For we are told that His banner over us is love. Are you displaying it, showing your love to Him by your love to others? showing the power of His love over you by your sweet, happy temper, and by trying to please Him always?

Carrying a banner means something. First, it means that you belong to or have to do with those whose banner you carry, and that you are not ashamed of them. At great Sunday-school festivals we know to which school a boy belongs by the flag that he carries. You would like to carry the flag of England or the Queen's royal flag, because you are English and loyal. So let us carry the banner of Jesus Christ because we are loyal to Him, and are not ashamed to own Him as our King. Secondly, it means that we are ready to fight, and ready to encourage others to fight under the same banner. When you are tempted to do something wrong, remember whose banner you carry, and do not disgrace it. If one does right, it makes it easier for the other to do right too. Thirdly, it means rejoicing. You know how flags are hung out on grand days, and carried in triumphal processions. The little hand that carries Christ's banner through His war, will carry it also in His triumph; the little hand that tries to unfurl it bravely now, will wave it when His glorious reign begins and His blessed kingdom is come. Then, "in the name of our God we will set up our banners" *now!*

"The Master hath cal ed us, the children who fear Him,
Who march 'neath Christ's banner, His own little band;
We love Him, and seek Him; we long to be near Him,
And rest in the light of His beautiful land."

24.

Twenty-fourth Day.

Soldiers.

"Chosen to be a soldier."—2 TIM. ii. 4.

ARE you a soldier? You ought to be, for you have been chosen to be a soldier in the glorious army of Jesus Christ.

You ought to be, for you have been "received into the congregation of Christ's flock" at your baptism, and engaged "manfully to fight under His banner against sin, the world, and the devil, and to continue Christ's faithful soldier and servant unto your life's end." You can never undo that, even if you are a deserter, and found in the enemy's ranks. The Captain of our salvation will not undo it, for He is ready to receive you, if you will but come and enlist now. Now, this very morning, come and enlist! This very morning ask Him to receive you into His noble army, and to give you first the shield of His salvation, and then the whole armor of God, and to "teach your hands to war and your fingers to fight," and to give you victories every day even now, and to let you share His grand triumphs hereafter.

Perhaps you know that you have enlisted already, you know and love your Captain, and He is enabling you, even if very feebly, yet really, to fight the good fight of faith? How came you to enlist? Was it any credit to you? Oh no! it was all His doing. It was He who chose you to be a soldier, not you who chose Him to be a Captain. And then He sent not some dreadful cannon roar, but the sweet bugle-call of His love to win you to join His ranks. And now He fights not only with you, but for you. In His war "nothing shall by any means hurt you," for "He was wounded" for you. Your life is safe with Him, for He laid down His own for you. By His side you can never be vanquished, because He goes forth "always conquering and to conquer."

"Stand up, stand up for Jesus!
Ye soldiers of the cross;
Lift high His royal banner,
It must not suffer loss.

"From victory to victory
His army shall be led,
Till every foe is vanquished,
And Christ is Lord indeed.

"Stand up, stand up for Jesus!
The trumpet call obey;
Forth to the mighty conflict,
In this His glorious day!"

25.

Twenty-fifth Day.

A Loyal Aim.

"That he may please him who hath chosen him to be a soldier."—2 TIM. ii. 4.

HERE is something worth aiming at, worth trying for! The Lord Jesus, the Captain of our salvation, is He who hath chosen us to be His soldiers; and now, does He only tell us that we may do our duty,—serve, obey, and fight? No; He tells us something more, gives us a hope and an aim so bright and pleasant, that it is like sunshine upon everything. He says, we "may *please* Him."

Only one who knows what it is to mourn for having grieved the dear Saviour, can quite understand what a happy word this is! That we, who have been cold, and careless, and sinful, grieving His love over and over again, should be told after all that we may *please* Him! Oh, if we love Him, our hearts will just leap at the hope of it! Perhaps we thought this could not be till we reached heaven; but you see His own word says, we "may please Him" now, while we are soldiers in the very midst of the fighting. St. Paul tells us one thing in which you may please Him: "Children, obey your parents in all things, for this is well-pleasing unto the Lord." But he prays too that the Colossians "might walk worthy of the Lord unto *all* pleasing."

Shall this be your aim and your hope to-day? Will you look up to the Lord Jesus now, and ask Him first to give you the faith without which "it is impossible to please Him," and then to show you "how you ought to walk and to please God," and so to help you to "do those things that are pleasing in His sight;" that all your ways, even every little step of your ways, may really and truly "please the Lord" (Prov. xvi. 7).

"True-hearted, whole-hearted, faithful, and loyal,
King of our lives, by Thy grace we will be;
Under Thy standard, exalted and royal,
Strong in Thy strength, we will battle for Thee.

"True-hearted, whole-hearted! Fullest allegiance,
Yielding henceforth to our glorious King,
Valiant endeavor and loving obedience,
Freely and joyously now we would bring."

Twenty-sixth Day. 26.

Obedience to Christ.

"Whatsoever He saith unto you, do it."—
JOHN ii. 5.

HOW are you to know what He says to you? Ah, it is so easy to know if we are really willing to know, and willing to obey when we do know! He has spoken so plainly to us in His word! In that He tells us, tells even little children, exactly what to do. It is most wonderful how He has said everything there for us, told us everything we ought to do. When you read a chapter or hear one read, listen and watch to see what He saith unto you in it. There is another way in which He tells us what to do. Do you not hear a little voice inside that always tells you to do the right thing, and not to do the wrong thing? That is conscience, and He speaks to you by it.

Another way is by those whom He has set over you. He has told you once for all to "obey your parents," and to "obey them that have the rule over you." So, when they tell you to do something, it is the Lord Jesus Himself that you have to obey in obeying them.

Now "whatsoever He saith unto you, do it!" Yes, "whatsoever," dear little one, whether easy or hard, do it because He tells you; do it for love of Him, and it will be a thousand times better and happier to obey your King than to please yourself. And He Himself will help you to do it; only look up to Him for grace to obey, and He will give it.

"Whatsoever He saith unto you, *do* it." Do not just think about doing it, or talk about doing it, but *do* it! "Do *it!*" Do the exact thing He would have you do, not something a little bit different, or something which you think will be very nearly the same, but do "*it.*"

And "do it" at once. It is so true, that "the very first moment is the easiest for obedience." Every minute that you put off doing the right thing makes it harder. Do not let your King have to "speak twice" to you. "Whatsoever He saith unto you, do it" cheerfully, exactly, and instantly.

"Jesus, help me, I am weak;
  Let me put my trust in Thee;
Teach me how and what to speak;
  Loving Saviour, care for me.
Dear Saviour, hear me,
  Hear a little child to-day;
Hear, oh hear me;
  Hear me when I pray."

Twenty-seventh Day. 27.

Do it Heartily.

"Whatsoever ye do, do it heartily, as to the Lord."—COL. iii. 23.

IN 2 Chron. xxxi. 21, we read of Hezekiah, that "in every work that he began, he did it with all his heart, and prospered." And this morning's "bell" rings a New Testament echo, "Do it heartily!" Sing it now, like a little peal of bells!

See if that does not ring in your ears all day, and remind you that it is not merely much pleasanter to be bright and brisk about everything, but that it is actually one of God's commands, written in His own word.

I know this is easier to some than to others. Perhaps it "comes natural" to you to do everything heartily. That is very nice, but it is not enough. What else? "Whatsoever ye do, do it heartily, *as unto the Lord*, and not unto men." He knows whether the industrious, energetic boy or girl is wishing to please Him, and looking up to Him for His smile; or whether He is forgotten all the while, and only the smile of others and the pleasure of being quick and busy is thought of. But perhaps it is hard to you to do things heartily. You like better to take your time, and so you dawdle, and do things in an idle way, especially what you do not much like doing. Is this right? Is it a little sin, when God's word says, "Whatsoever ye do, do it heartily!"

Is it not just as much disobeying God as breaking any other command? Are you not *guilty* before Him? Very likely you never thought of it in this way, but there the words stand, and neither you nor I can alter them. First ask Him to forgive you all the past idleness and idle ways, for Christ's sake, and then ask Him to give you strength henceforth to obey this word of His. And then listen to the little chime, "Do it heartily! do it heartily!" And *then* the last word of the verse about Hezekiah will be true of you too—"Prospered!"

"Up and doing, little Christian!
Up and doing, while 'tis day!
Do the work the Master gives you,
Do not loiter by the way.
For we all have work before us,
You, dear child, as well as I;
Let us learn to seek our duty,
And to 'do it heartily.'"

Twenty-eighth Day. 28.

The Sight of Faith.

"As seeing Him who is invisible."—
HEB. xi. 27.

IF we were always doing everything just as if we saw Him, whom having not seen we love, how different our lives would be! How much happier too! How brave, and bright, and patient we should be, if all the time we could really see Jesus as Stephen saw Him! And by faith, the precious faith which God is ready to give to all who ask, we may go on our way with this light upon it, "as seeing Him who is invisible."

These words were said of Moses; and this seeing Him by faith had three effects. First, "he forsook Egypt;" it made him ready to give up anything for his God, and God's people. It made him true and loyal to God's cause. What did He care for anything else, so long as he saw "Him who is invisible?" Secondly, it took away all his fear. What was "the wrath of the king" to him, when Jehovah was by his side? Of what should he be afraid? Thirdly, it enabled him to "endure," to wait patiently for forty years in the desert, and then to work patiently for forty years in the wilderness; and only think how strength-giving that sight of faith must be which enabled him to endure everything for eighty years!

Try for yourself to-day what was such great and long help to Moses. Ask God, before you go down-stairs, for faith, "the eye of the soul," so that you may walk all day long "as seeing Him who is invisible." When you are tempted to indulge in something wrong,—idleness, or carlessness, or selfishness,—this will help you to give it up at once, and forsake it; for how can you give way to it when your eye meets His? When something makes you afraid, this will make you brave and peaceful; for how can you fear anything when your God is so near? When lessons, or work, or even having to be quiet with nothing to do, seem very tiresome, and you are tempted to be impatient, and perhaps cross, this will help you to endure, and not only so, but to feel patient; for how can you be impatient when you are looking up to Him, and He is looking down on you all the time!

"God will not leave me all alone,
He never will forsake His own;
When not another friend I see,
The Lord is looking down on me."

Twenty-Ninth Day.

29.

No Weights.

"Let us lay aside every weight."—HEB. xii. 1.

IF you were going to run a race, you would first put down all the parcels you might have been carrying. And if you had a heavy little parcel in your pocket, you would take that out, and lay it down too, because it would hinder you in running. You would know better than to say, "I will put down the parcels which I have in my hands, but nobody can see the one in my pocket, so that one won't matter!" You would "lay aside *every* weight."

You have a race to run to-day, a little piece of the great race that is set before you. God has set a splendid prize before you, "the prize of the high calling of God in Christ Jesus," a crown that is incorruptible.

Now what are you going to do about the weights, the things that hinder you from running this race? You know some things do seem to hinder you; will you keep them or lay them aside? Will you only lay aside something that every one can see is hindering you, so that you will get a little credit for putting it down, and keep something that your own little conscience knows is a real hindrance, though no one else knows anything at all about it? Oh, take St. Paul's wise and holy advice, and make up your mind to lay aside *every* weight.

Different persons have different weights; we must find out what ours are, and give them up. One finds that if she does not get up directly she is called, the time slips by, and there is not enough left for quiet prayer and Bible-reading. Then here is a little weight that must be laid aside. Another is at school, and finds that he gets no good, but a little harm, when he goes much with a certain boy. Then he must lay that weight aside. Another takes a story-book up to bed, and reads it while nurse is brushing her hair, and up to the last minute, and then her head is so full of the story that she only *says words* when she kneels down, and can not really *pray* at all. Can she doubt that this is a weight which must be laid aside?

It may seem hard to lay our pet weight down; but oh, if you only knew how light we feel when it is laid down, and how much easier it is to run the race which God has set before us!

Thirtieth Day.

30.

The Shield of Salvation.

"Thou hast also given me the shield of Thy salvation."—2 SAM. xxii. 36.

THIS beautiful little text teaches us a very precious truth. It shows us that the salvation which the Lord Jesus came to bring is not only salvation at last, just escaping hell, but that it is salvation now, and salvation in everything. Salvation does not only mean victory at last, but it is like a broad, shining shield, given to us in the midst of the battle, coming between us and the poisoned arrows and sharp sword-thrusts of the enemy. It is a shield not only to keep us from death, but to keep us from being hurt and wounded.

It is the shield which the Captain *has* given us to use now, as well as the crown which He *will* give when the warfare is ended.

How are you to use this shield? what does it really mean for you? It means, that if you have come to the Lord Jesus to be saved, He does not merely say He *will* save you, but that you *are* saved, that He saves you now. And this is how you are to use it—believe it, and be sure of it, because you have His word for it; and then, when a temptation comes, tell the enemy that he has nothing to do with you, for you are saved; that you belong to Jesus, and not to him,—look up and say, "Jesus saves me!" Will He fail you? Did He ever let any find themselves deceived and mistaken who looked up in faith and confidence to Him, trusting in His great salvation? Never! and never will you find this shield of His salvation fail to cover you completely. Satan himself can not touch you when you are behind this shield! Lift it up when you see him coming, even ever so far off, and you will be safe.

"Jesus saves me every day,
    Jesus saves me every night;
Jesus saves me all the way,
    Through the darkness, through the light."

Thirty-first Day.

31.

I will love Thee.

"I will love Thee, O Lord."—Ps. xviii. 1.

YES, even if I have never loved Thee before, I will love Thee, O Lord, now!

I will love Thee, Lord Jesus, because Thou hast loved me, and because Thou art loving me now, and wilt love me to the end. Oh, forgive me for not having loved Thee! How could I have helped loving Thee, when Thou wast waiting all the time for me, waiting so patiently while I did not care about Thee! Oh, forgive me! and now I will love Thee always; for Thou wilt take my love, and fix it on Thyself, and keep it for Thyself.

I will love Thee, O Lord Jesus; I will not listen to Satan, who tries to keep me from loving Thee; I will not ask myself anything about it, lest I should begin to get puzzled about whether I do love Thee or not. Thou knowest that I do want to love Thee; and now, dear Lord Jesus, hear me say that I *will* love Thee, and that I will trust Thee to make me love Thee more and more, always more and more.

I have said it, dear Lord Jesus, and Thou hast heard me say it. And I am so glad I have said it. I do not want ever to take it back, and Thou wilt not let me take it back. I am to love Thee always now; and Thou wilt give me Thy Holy Spirit to shed abroad Thy love in my heart, so that it may be filled with love. Fill me so full of Thy love that it may run over into everything I do, and that I may love everybody, because I love Thee.

Yes, I will love Thee, dear Lord Jesus!

"My Saviour, I love Thee, I know Thou art mine!
For Thee all the follies of sin I resign;
My gracious Redeemer, my Saviour art Thou;
If ever I loved Thee, my Saviour, 'tis now!

'I love Thee, because Thou hast first lovèd me,
And purchased my pardon on Calvary's tree;
I love Thee for wearing the thorns on Thy brow;
If ever I loved Thee, my Saviour, 'tis now!

"I will love Thee in life, I will love Thee in death,
And praise Thee as long as Thou lendest me breath:
And say, when the death-dew lies cold on my brow,
If ever I loved Thee, my Saviour, 'tis now!"

SGCB Classic Reprints

Biblical & Theological Studies by the faculty of Princeton Seminary from 1912 was published in commemoration of the 100th anniversary of Princeton. Warfield, Machen, Vos, Allis, Hodge Jr., and ten other giants contribute to this timeless book.

Sermons to the Natural & Spiritual Man by W.G.T. Shedd are two volumes that speak to both the converted and unconverted. A.A. Hodge said, "If not absolutely the best, yet of the very best doctrinal and spiritual sermons produced in this generation."

A History of Preaching by Edwin Charles Dargan is a two volume hardcover set that is the standard work of its kind in the field of Homiletics. Every pastor, student and teacher of religion should own it.

Homiletics and Pastoral Theology by W.G.T. Shedd expounds almost every aspect of preaching, analyzing its nature, outlining the main features which should characterize powerful preaching. The second part is devoted to the vital subject of Pastoral Theology. Briefer but equally valuable.

The Power of God unto Salvation by B.B. Warfield is the hundredth anniversary edition of Warfield's first volume of sermons. This volume includes a warmly written Preface by Sinclair Ferguson, and an Appendix of Four Hymns and Eleven Religious Poems written by Warfield.

Christ in Song: Hymns of Immanuel from all ages compiled by Philip Schaff drew forth the following high praise from Charles Hodge, "After all, apart from the Bible, the best antidote to all these false theories of the person and work of Christ, is such a book as Dr. Schaff's 'Christ in Song.'"

The Shorter Catechism Illustrated, from Christian Biography & History *by John Whitercoss first appeared in 1828 and passed through many editions.* It last appeared in the 1968 edition done by Banner of Truth.

The Lord of Glory by B.B. Warfield is considered one of the most thorough defenses of the Deity of Christ ever written. Over 320 pages of exposition of the designations used of our Lord throughout the New Testament.

First Things by Gardiner Spring is a two volume work setting forth the foundation laid for mankind in the opening chapters of Genesis. Very Rare!

The Preacher and His Models by James Stalker is the substance of the Yale Lectures of Preaching from 1891. This gifted Scots preacher uses both the Prophets and Apostles to stimulate modern preachers of the Gospel.

Imago Christi: The Example of Jesus Christ by James Stalker was called by C.H. Spurgeon *"an immortal book."* Our Lord is presented as a model for every aspect of life in this world of sin and misery. Thoroughly evangelical!

The Church Member's Guide by John Angell James was once the most popular book in both the UK and the USA for instructing Christian's in their privileges and responsibilities as members of the body of Christ.

Young Lady's Guide: to the Harmonious Development of Christian Character by Harvey Newcomb sets forth the biblical foundation needed for a young lady to grow to Christian womanhood. A timeless masterpiece.

Call us toll free **1-877-666-9469**
E-mail us at **sgcb@charter.net**
Visit us on the web at **solid-ground-books.com**

CPSIA information can be obtained at www.ICGtesting.com
Printed in the USA
LVOW122039081211

258538LV00001B/1/A